YOUR

HO[

2016

AQUARIUS

YOUR PERSONAL HOROSCOPE 2016

AQUARIUS

21st January–19th February

igloobooks

Published in 2015
by Igloo Books Ltd
Cottage Farm
Sywell
NN6 0BJ
www.igloobooks.com

Cover images: Thinkstock / Getty

HUN001 0715
2 4 6 8 10 9 7 5 3 1
ISBN 978-1-78440-580-9

This is an abridged version of material originally published
in Old Moore's Horoscope and Astral Diary.

Printed and manufactured in China

CONTENTS

INTRODUCTION

Your Personal Horoscopes have been specifically created to allow you to get the most from astrological patterns and the way they have a bearing on not only your zodiac sign, but nuances within it. Using the diary section of the book you can read about the influences and possibilities of each and every day of the year. It will be possible for you to see when you are likely to be cheerful and happy or those times when your nature is in retreat and you will be more circumspect. The diary will help to give you a feel for the specific 'cycles' of astrology and the way they can subtly change your day-to-day life. For example, when you see the sign ☿, this means that the planet Mercury is retrograde at that time. Retrograde means it appears to be running backwards through the zodiac. Such a happening has a significant effect on communication skills, but this is only one small aspect of how the Personal Horoscope can help you.

With Your Personal Horoscope the story doesn't end with the diary pages. It includes simple ways for you to work out which zodiac sign was occupied by the Moon at the time of your birth, and what this means for your personality. In addition, if you know the time of day you were born, it is possible to discover your Ascendant, yet another important guide to your personal make-up and potential.

Many readers are interested in relationships and in knowing how well they get on with people of other astrological signs. You might also be interested in the way you appear to other people. If you are such a person, the section on Venus will be of particular interest. Despite the rapidly changing position of this planet, you can work out your Venus sign, and learn what bearing it will have on your life.

Using Your Personal Horoscope, you can travel on one of the most fascinating and rewarding journeys that anyone can take – the journey to a better realisation of self.

THE ESSENCE OF AQUARIUS

Exploring the Personality of Aquarius the Water Carrier

(21ST JANUARY–19TH FEBRUARY)

What's in a sign?

Oh, what a wonderful person you can be! Despite a number of contradictions and one of the most complicated natures to be found anywhere in the zodiac, you certainly know how to make friends and influence people. Your ruling planet is Uranus, one of the more recently discovered members of the solar system's family. It rules modern communications, such as radio and television, and also has a response to the recent discoveries of science. It is within the world of 'the modern' that you reside and you have little or no difficulty keeping up with the ever-increasing pace of life.

People naturally like you and it's not surprising. You are open, liberal, and rarely judgmental, and you are often surrounded by deeply original and even eccentric types. Life to you is a storybook full of fascinating tales. Aquarians amass information 'on the hoof' and very little passes you by. Understanding what makes others tick is meat and drink to you and proves to be a source of endless joy. Unlike the other Air signs of Gemini and Libra, you are able to spend long hours on your own if necessary and always keep your mind active.

Aquarians have great creative potential: they are refined, often extremely well educated and they remain totally classless. This makes it easy for you to get on with just about any sort of person and also explains your general success in the material world. You are fascinating, original, thought-provoking and even quite deep on occasions. Matters that take months for others to synthesise, you can absorb in minutes. It is clear to everyone that you are one of life's natural leaders, but when you head any organisation you do so by co-operation and example because you are not in the least authoritarian.

In love you can be ardent and sincere – for a while at least. You need to be loved and it's true that deeply personal relationships can be a problem if they are not supplying what is most important to you. Few people know the real you, because your nature exists on so many different levels. For this reason alone you defy analysis and tend to remain outside the scope of orthodoxy. And because people can't weigh you up adequately, you appear to be more fascinating than ever.

Aquarius resources

Your chief resource has to be originality. Like a precious Fabergé egg you are a single creation, unique and quite unlike anything else to be found anywhere in the world. Of course, used wrongly, this can make you seem odd or even downright peculiar. But Aquarians usually have a knack for creating the best possible impression. The chances are that you dress in your own way and speak the words that occur to you, and that you have a side to your nature that shuns convention. Despite this you know how to adapt when necessary. As a result your dinner parties include guests of a wide variety of types and stations. All of these people think they know the 'real you' and remain committed to helping you as much as they can.

The natural adaptability that goes along with being an Aquarian makes it possible for you to turn your hand to many different projects. And because you are from an Air sign, you can undertake a variety of tasks at the same time. This makes for a busy life, but being on the go is vital for you and you only tire when you are forced into jobs that you find demeaning, pointless or downright dull.

All of the above combines to make a nature that has 'resourcefulness' as its middle name. Arriving at a given set of circumstances – say a specific task that has to be undertaken – you first analyse what is required. Having done so you get cracking and invariably manage to impress all manner of people with your dexterity, attention to detail and downright intelligence. You can turn work into a social event, or derive financial gain from your social life. Activity is the keyword and you don't really differentiate between the various components of life as many people would.

Success depends on a number of different factors. You need to be doing things you enjoy as much as you can and you simply cannot be held back or bound to follow rules that appear to make no sense to you. You respond well to kindness, and generally receive it because you are so considerate yourself. But perhaps your greatest skill of all is your ability to make a silk purse out of a sow's ear. You are never stuck for an idea and rarely let financial restrictions get in your way.

Beneath the surface

'What you see is what you get' could never really be considered a sensible or accurate statement when applied to the sign of Aquarius. It's difficult enough for you to know the way your complicated mind works, and almost impossible for others to sort out the tangle of possibilities. Your mind can be as untidy as a tatty workbox on occasions and yet at other times you can see through situations with a clarity that would dazzle almost any observer. It really depends on a whole host of circumstances, some of which are inevitably beyond your own control. You are at your best when you are allowed to take charge from the very start of any project, because then your originality of thought comes into play. Your sort of logic is unique to you, so don't expect anyone else to go down the same mental routes that you find easy to follow.

Aquarians are naturally kind and don't tend to discriminate. This is not a considered matter, it's simply the way you are. As a result it is very hard for you to understand prejudice, or individuals who show any form of intolerance. The fairness that you exemplify isn't something that you have to work at – it comes as naturally to you as breathing does.

You can be very peculiar and even a little cranky on occasions. These aspects of your nature are unlikely to have any bearing on your overall popularity, but they do betray a rather unusual mindset that isn't like that of any other zodiac sign. When you feel stressed you tend to withdraw into yourself, which is not really good for you. A much better strategy would be to verbalise what you are thinking, even though this is not always particularly easy to do.

There are many people in the world who think they know you well, but each and every one of them knows only one Aquarian. There are always more, each a unique individual and probably as much of a mystery to you as they would be to all your relatives and friends, that is if any of them suspected just how deep and mysterious you can be. Despite these facts, your mind is clear and concise, enabling you to get to the truth of any given situation almost immediately. You should never doubt your intuitive foresight and, in the main, must always back your hunches. It is rare indeed for you to be totally wrong about the outcome of any potential situation and your genuine originality of thought is the greatest gift providence has bestowed on you.

Making the best of yourself

Interacting with the world is most important to you. Although you can sometimes be a good deal quieter than the other Air signs of Gemini and Libra, you are still a born communicator, with a great need to live your life to the full. If you feel hemmed in or constrained by circumstances, you are not going to show your best face to family, friends or colleagues. That's why you must move heaven and earth to make certain that you are not tied down in any way. Maintaining a sense of freedom is really just a mental state to Aquarius but it is absolutely vital to your well-being.

As far as work is concerned you need to be doing something that allows you the room you need to move. Any occupation that means thinking on your feet would probably suit you fine. All the same you feel more comfortable in administrative surroundings, rather than getting your hands dirty. Any profession that brings change and variety on a daily basis would be best. You are a good team operator, and yet can easily lead from the front. Don't be frightened to show colleagues that you have an original way of looking at life and that you are an inveterate problem solver.

In terms of friendship, you tend to be quite catholic in your choice of pals. Making the best of yourself means keeping things that way. You are not naturally jealous yourself, but you do tend to attract friends who are. Make it plain that you can't tie yourself down to any one association, no matter how old or close it may be. At least if you do this nobody can suggest that they weren't warned when you wander off to talk to someone else. Personal relationships are a different matter, though it's hardly likely that you would live in the pocket of your partner. In any situation you need space to breathe, and this includes romantic attachments. People who know you well will not try to hem you in.

Don't be frightened to show your unconventional – even wild – side to the world at large. You are a bold character, with a great deal to say and a natural warmth that could melt an iceberg. This is the way providence made you and it is only right to use your gifts to the full.

The impressions you give

You are not a naturally secretive person and don't hold back very much when it comes to speaking your mind. It might be suggested therefore that the external and internal Aquarian is more or less the same person. Although generally true, it has to be remembered that you have a multi-faceted nature and one that adapts quickly to changing circumstances. It is this very adaptability that sets you apart in the eyes of the world.

You often make decisions based on intuitive foresight and although many Aquarians are of above average intelligence, you won't always make use of a deep knowledge of any given situation. In essence you often do what seems right, though you tend to act whilst others are still standing around and thinking. This makes you good to have around in a crisis and convinces many of those looking on that you are incredibly capable, relaxed and confident. Of course this isn't always the case, but even a nervous interior tends to breed outward action in the case of your zodiac sign, so the world can be forgiven for jumping to the wrong conclusion.

People like you – there's no doubt about that. However, you must realise that you have a very upfront attitude, which on occasions is going to get you into trouble. Your occasional weirdness, rather than being a turn-off, is likely to stimulate the interest that the world has in you. Those with whom you come into contact invariably find your personality to be attractive, generous, high-spirited and refreshing. For all these reasons it is very unlikely that you would actually make many enemies, even if some folk are clearly jealous of the easy way you have with the world.

One of the great things about Aquarians is that they love to join in. As a result you may find yourself doing all sorts of things that others would find either difficult or frightening. You can be zany, wild and even mad on occasions, but these tendencies will only get you liked all the more. The world will only tire of you if you allow yourself to get down in the dumps or grumpy – a very rare state for Aquarius.

The way forward

In terms of living your life to the full, it is probable that you don't need any real advice from an astrologer. Your confidence allows you to go places that would make some people shiver, whilst your intuitive foresight gives you the armoury you need to deal with a world that can sometimes seem threatening. Yet for all this you are not immune to mental turmoil on occasions, and probably spend rather too much time in the fast lane. It's good to rest, a fact that you need to remember the next time you find yourself surrounded by twenty-seven jobs, all of which you are trying to undertake at the same time.

The more the world turns in the direction of information technology, the happier you are likely to become. If others have difficulty in this age of computers, it's likely that you relish the challenges and the opportunities that these artificial intelligences offer. You are happy with New Age concepts and tend to look at the world with compassion and understanding. Despite the fact that you are always on the go, it's rare for you to be moving forward so fast that you forget either the planet that brought you to birth, or the many underprivileged people who inhabit parts of it. You have a highly developed conscience and tend to work for the good of humanity whenever you can.

You might not be constructed of the highest moral fibre known to humanity, a fact that sometimes shows when it comes to romantic attachments. Many Aquarians play the field at some time in their lives and it's certain that you need a personal relationship that keeps you mentally stimulated. Although your exterior can sometimes seem superficial, you have a deep and sensitive soul – so perhaps you should marry a poet, or at least someone who can cope with the twists and turns of the Aquarian mind. Aquarians who tie themselves down too early, or to the wrong sort of individual, invariable end up regretting the fact.

You can be deeply creative and need to live in clean and cheerful surroundings. Though not exactly a minimalist you don't like clutter and constantly need to spring-clean your home – and your mind. Living with others isn't difficult for you, in fact it's essential. Since you are so adaptable you fit in easily to almost any environment, though you will always ultimately stamp your own character onto it. You love to be loved and offer a great deal in return, even if you are occasionally absent when people need you the most. In essence you are in love with life and so perhaps you should not be too surprised to discover that it is very fond of you too.

AQUARIUS ON THE CUSP

Astrological profiles are altered for those people born at either the beginning or the end of a zodiac sign, or, more properly, on the cusps of a sign. In the case of Aquarius this would be on the 21st of January and for two or three days after, and similarly at the end of the sign, probably from the 17th to the 19th of February.

The Capricorn Cusp – January 21st to 23rd

What really sets you apart is a genuinely practical streak that isn't always present in the sign of Aquarius when taken alone. You are likely to have all the joy of life and much of the devil-may-care attitude of your Sun sign, but at the same time you are capable of getting things done in a very positive way. This makes you likely to achieve a higher degree of material success and means that you ally managerial skills with the potential for rolling up your sleeves and taking part in the 'real work' yourself. Alongside this you are able to harness the naturally intuitive qualities of Aquarius in a very matter-of-fact way. Few people would have the ability to pull the wool over your eyes and you are rarely stuck for a solution, even to apparently difficult problems.

You express yourself less well than Aquarius taken alone, and you may have a sort of reserve that leads others to believe that your mind is full of still waters which run very deep. The air of mystery can actually be quite useful, because it masks an ability to react and move quickly when necessary, which is a great surprise to the people around you. However, there are two sides to every coin and if there is a slightly negative quality to this cuspid position it might lie in the fact that you are not quite the communicator that tends to be the case with Aquarius, and you could go through some fairly quiet and introspective phases that those around you find somewhat difficult to understand. In a positive sense this offers a fairly wistful aspect to your nature that may, in romantic applications, appear very attractive. There is something deeply magnetic about your nature and it isn't quite possible for everyone to understand what makes you tick. Actually this is part of your appeal because there is nothing like curiosity on the part of others to enhance your profile.

Getting things done is what matters the most to you, harnessed to the ability to see the wider picture in life. It's true that not everyone understands your complex nature, but in friendship you are scarcely short of supportive types. Family members can be especially important to you and personal attachments are invariably made for life.

The Pisces Cusp – February 17th to 19th

It appears that you are more of a thinker than most and achieve depths of contemplation that would be totally alien to some signs of the zodiac. Much of your life is given over to the service you show for humanity as a whole but you don't sink into the depths of despair in the way that some Piscean individuals are inclined to do. You are immensely likeable and rarely stuck for a good idea. You know how to enjoy yourself, even if this quality is usually tied to the support and assistance that you constantly give to those around you.

Many of you will already have chosen a profession that somehow fulfils your need to be of service, and it isn't unusual for Pisces-cusp Aquarians to alter their path in life totally if it isn't fulfilling this most basic requirement. When necessary, you can turn your hand to almost anything, generally giving yourself totally to the task in hand, sometimes to the exclusion of everything else. People with this combination often have two very different sorts of career, sometimes managing to do both at the same time. Confidence in practical matters isn't usually lacking, even if you sometimes think that your thought processes are a little bit muddled.

In love you are ardent and more sincere than Aquarius sometimes seems to be. There can be a tinge of jealousy at work now and again in deep relationships, but you are less likely than Pisces to let this show. You tend to be very protective of the people who are most important in your life and these are probably fewer in number than often seems to be the case for Aquarius. Your love of humanity and the needs it has of you are of supreme importance and you barely let a day pass without offering some sort of assistance. For this reason, and many others, you are a much loved individual and show your most caring face to the world for the majority of your life. Material success can be hard to come by at first, but it isn't really an aspect of life that worries you too much in any case. It is far more important for you to be content with your lot and, if you are happy, it seems that more or less everything else tends to follow.

AQUARIUS AND ITS ASCENDANTS

The nature of every individual on the planet is composed of the rich variety of zodiac signs and planetary positions that were present at the time of their birth. Your Sun sign, which in your case is Aquarius, is one of the many factors when it comes to assessing the unique person you are. Probably the most important consideration, other than your Sun sign, is to establish the zodiac sign that was rising over the eastern horizon at the time that you were born. This is your Ascending or Rising sign. Most popular astrology fails to take account of the Ascendant, and yet its importance remains with you from the very moment of your birth, through every day of your life. The Ascendant is evident in the way you approach the world, and so, when meeting a person for the first time, it is this astrological influence that you are most likely to notice first. Our Ascending sign essentially represents what we appear to be, while the Sun sign is what we feel inside ourselves.

The Ascendant also has the potential for modifying our overall nature. For example, if you were born at a time of day when Aquarius was passing over the eastern horizon (this would be around the time of dawn) then you would be classed as a double Aquarian. As such, you would typify this zodiac sign, both internally and in your dealings with others. However, if your Ascendant sign turned out to be a Fire sign, such as Aries, there would be a profound alteration of nature, away from the expected qualities of Aquarius.

One of the reasons why popular astrology often ignores the Ascendant is that it has always been rather difficult to establish. We have found a way to make this possible by devising an easy-to-use table, which you will find on page 157 of this book. Using this, you can establish your Ascendant sign at a glance. You will need to know your rough time of birth, then it is simply a case of following the instructions.

For those readers who have no idea of their time of birth it might be worth allowing a good friend, or perhaps your partner, to read through the section that follows this introduction. Someone who deals with you on a regular basis may easily discover your Ascending sign, even though you could have some difficulty establishing it for yourself. A good understanding of this component of your nature is essential if you want to be aware of that 'other person' who is responsible for the way you make contact with the world at large. Your Sun sign, Ascendant sign, and the other pointers in this book will, together, allow you a far better understanding of what makes you tick as an individual. Peeling back the different layers of your astrological make-up can be an enlightening experience, and the Ascendant may represent one of the most important layers of all.

Aquarius with Aquarius Ascendant

You are totally unique and quite original, so much so that very few people could claim to understand what makes you tick. Routines get on your nerves and you need to be out there doing something most of the time. Getting where you want to go in life isn't too difficult, except that when you arrive, your destination might not look half so interesting as it did before. You are well liked and should have many friends. This is not to say that your pals have much in common with each other, because you choose from a wide cross-section of people. Although folks see you as being very reasonable in the main, you are capable of being quite cranky on occasions. Your intuition is extremely strong and is far less likely to let you down than would be the case with some individuals.

Travel is very important to you and you will probably live for some time in a different part of your own country, or even in another part of the world. At work you are more than capable, but do need something to do that you find personally stimulating, because you are not very good at constant routine. You can be relied upon to use your originality and find solutions that are instinctive and brilliant. Most people are very fond of you.

Aquarius with Pisces Ascendant

Here we find the originality of Aquarius balanced by the very sensitive qualities of Pisces, and it makes for a very interesting combination. When it comes to understanding other people you are second to none, but it's certain that you are more instinctive than either Pisces or Aquarius when taken alone. You are better at routines than Aquarius, but also relish a challenge more than the typical Piscean would. Active and enterprising, you tend to know what you want from life, but consideration for others, and the world at large, will always be part of the scenario. People with this combination often work on behalf of humanity and are to be found in social work, the medical profession and religious institutions. As far as beliefs are concerned you don't conform to established patterns, and yet may get closer to the truth of the Creator than many deep theological thinkers have ever been able to. Acting on impulse as much as you do means that not everyone understands the way your mind works, but your popularity will invariably see you through.

Passionate and deeply sensitive, you are able to negotiate the twists and turns of a romantic life that is hardly likely to be run-of-the-mill. In the end, however, you should be able to discover a very deep personal and spiritual happiness.

Aquarius with Aries Ascendant

If ever anyone could be accused of setting off immediately, but slowly, it has to be you. These are very contradictory signs and the differences will express themselves in a variety of ways. One thing is certain, you have tremendous tenacity and will see a job through patiently from beginning to end, without tiring on the way and ensuring that every detail is taken care of properly. This combination often brings good health and a great capacity for continuity, particularly in terms of the length of life. You are certainly not as argumentative as the typical Aries, but you do know how to get your own way, which is just as well because you are usually thinking on behalf of everyone else and not just on your own account.

At home you can relax, which is a blessing for Aries, though in fact you seldom choose to do so because you always have some project or other on the go. You probably enjoy knocking down and rebuilding walls, though this is a practical tendency and not responsive to relationships, in which you are ardent and sincere. Impetuosity is as close to your heart as is the case for any type of subject, though you certainly have the ability to appear patient and steady. But it's just a front, isn't it?

Aquarius with Taurus Ascendant

There is nothing that you fail to think about deeply and with great intensity. You are wise, honest and very scientific in your approach to life. Routines are necessary in life but you have most of them sorted out well in advance and so always have time to look at the next interesting fact. If you don't spend all your time watching documentaries, you make a good friend and love to socialise. Most of the great discoveries of the world were probably made by people with this sort of astrological combination, though your nature is rather 'odd' on occasions and so can be rather difficult for others to understand.

You may be most surprised when others tell you that you are eccentric, but you don't really mind too much because for half of the time you are not inhabiting the same world as the rest of us. Because you can be delightfully dotty you are probably much loved and cherished by your friends, of which there are likely to be many. Family members probably adore you too, and you can be guaranteed to entertain anyone with whom you come into contact. The only fly in the ointment is that you sometimes lose track of reality, whatever that might be, and fly high in your own atmosphere of rarefied possibilities.

Aquarius with Gemini Ascendant

If you were around in the 1960s there is every chance that you were the first to go around with flowers in your hair. You are unconventional, original, quirky and entertaining. Few people would fail to notice your presence and you take life as it comes, even though on most occasions you are firmly in the driving seat. In all probability you care very much about the planet on which you live and the people with whom you share it. Not everyone understands you, but that does not really matter, for you have more than enough communication skills to put your message across intact. You should avoid wearing yourself out by worrying about things that you cannot control, and you definitely gain from taking time out to meditate. However, whether or not you allow yourself that luxury remains to be seen.

If you are not the most communicative form of Gemini subject then you must come a close second. Despite this fact, much of what you have to say makes real sense and you revel in the company of interesting, intelligent and stimulating people, whose opinions on a host of matters will add to your own considerations. You are a true original in every sense of the word and the mere fact of your presence in the world is bound to add to the enjoyment of life experienced by the many people with whom you make contact.

Aquarius with Cancer Ascendant

The truly original spark, for which the sign of Aquarius is famed, can only enhance the caring qualities of Cancer, and is also inclined to bring the Crab out of its shell to a much greater extent than would be the case with certain other zodiac combinations. Aquarius is a party animal and never arrives without something interesting to say, which is doubly the case when the reservoir of emotion and consideration from Cancer is feeding the tap. Your nature can be rather confusing for even you to deal with, but you are inspirational, bright, charming and definitely fun to be around.

The Cancer element in your nature means that you care about your home and the people to whom you are related. You are also a good and loyal friend, who would keep attachments for much longer than could be expected for Aquarius alone. You love to travel and can be expected to make many journeys to far-off places during your life. Some attention will have to be paid to your health, because you are capable of burning up masses of nervous energy, often without getting the periods of rest and contemplation that are essential to the deeper qualities of the sign of Cancer. Nevertheless you have determination, resilience and a refreshing attitude that lifts the spirits of the people in your vicinity.

Aquarius with Leo Ascendant

All associations with Aquarius bring originality, and you are no exception. You aspire to do your best most of the time but manage to achieve your objectives in an infinitely amusing and entertaining way. Not that you set out to do so, because if you are an actor on the stage of life, it seems as though you are a natural one. There is nothing remotely pretentious about your breezy personality or your ability to occupy the centre of any stage. This analogy is quite appropriate because you probably like the theatre. Being in any situation when reality is suspended for a while suits you down to the ground, and in any case you may regularly ask yourself if you even recognise what reality is. Always asking questions, both of yourself and the world at large, you soldier on relentlessly, though not to the exclusion of having a good time on the way.

Keeping to tried and tested paths is not your way. You are a natural trailblazer who is full of good ideas and who has the energy to put them into practice. You care deeply for the people who play an important part in your life but are wise enough to allow them the space they need to develop their own personalities along the way. Most people like you, many love you, and one or two think that you really are the best thing since sliced bread.

Aquarius with Virgo Ascendant

How could anyone make the convention, unconventional? Well, if anyone can manage it, you can. There are great contradictions here, because on the one hand you always want to do the expected thing but, on the other hand, the Aquarian quality within your nature loves to surprise everyone on the way. If you don't always know what you are thinking or doing, it's a pretty safe bet that others won't either, so it's important on occasions to really stop and think. However this is not a pressing concern, because you tend to live a fairly happy life and muddle through no matter what. Other people tend to take to you well and it is likely that you will have many friends. You tend to be bright and cheerful and can approach even difficult tasks with the certainty that you have the skills necessary to see them through to their conclusion. Give and take are important factors in the life of any individual and particularly so in your case. Because you can stretch yourself in order to understand what makes other people think and act in the way that they do, you have the reputation of being a good friend and a reliable colleague.

In love you can be somewhat more fickle than the typical Virgoan, and yet you are always interesting to live with. Where you are, things happen, and you mix a sparkling wit with deep insights.

Aquarius with Libra Ascendant

Stand by for a truly interesting and very inspiring combination here, but one that is sometimes rather difficult to fathom, even for the sort of people who believe themselves to be very perceptive. The reason for this could be that any situation has to be essentially fixed and constant in order to get a handle on it, and this is certainly not the case for the Aquarian–Libran type. The fact is that both these signs are Air signs, and to a certain extent as unpredictable as the wind itself.

To most people you seem to be original, frank, free and very outspoken. Not everything you do makes sense to others, for you are a free-thinking idealist at heart. With age you mature somewhat, but never too much, because you will always see the strange, the comical and the original in life. This is what keeps you young and is one of the factors that makes you very attractive to others. Many people will want to 'adopt' you and you are at your very best when in company. Much of your effort is expounded on others and yet, unless you discipline yourself a good deal, personal relationships of the romantic sort can bring certain difficulties. Careful planning is necessary.

Aquarius with Scorpio Ascendant

Here we have a combination that shows much promise and a flexibility that allows many changes in direction, allied to a power to succeed, sometimes very much against all the odds. Aquarius lightens the load of the Scorpio mind, turning the depths into potential, and intuitive foresight into a means for getting on in life. There are depths here, because even airy Aquarius isn't so easy to understand, and it is therefore a fact that some people with this combination will always be something of a mystery. However, even this fact can be turned to your advantage because it means that people will always be looking at you. Confidence is so often the key to success in life and the Scorpio–Aquarius mix offers this, or at least appears to do so. Even when this is not entirely the case, the fact that everyone around you believes it to be true is often enough.

You are usually good to know, and show a keen intellect and a deep intelligence, aided by a fascination for life that knows no bounds. When at your best you are giving, understanding, balanced and active. On those occasions when things are not going well for you, beware of a stubborn streak and the need to be sensational. Keep it light and happy and you won't go far wrong.

Aquarius with Sagittarius Ascendant

There is an original streak to your nature which is very attractive to the people with whom you share your life. Always different, ever on the go and anxious to try out the next experiment in life, you are interested in almost everything, and yet deeply attached to almost nothing. Everyone you know thinks that you are a little 'odd', but you probably don't mind them believing this because you know it to be true. In fact it is possible that you positively relish your eccentricity, which sets you apart from the common herd and means that you are always going to be noticed.

Although it may seem strange with this combination of Air and Fire, you can be distinctly cool on occasions, have a deep and abiding love of your own company now and again and won't be easily understood. Love comes fairly easily to you but there are times when you are accused of being self-possessed, self-indulgent and not willing enough to fall in line with the wishes of those around you. Despite this, you walk on and on down your own path. At heart you are an extrovert and you love to party, often late into the night. Luxury appeals to you, though it tends to be of the transient sort. Travel could easily play a major and a very important part in your life.

Aquarius with Capricorn Ascendant

Here the determination of Capricorn is assisted by a slightly more adaptable quality and an off-beat personality that tends to keep everyone else guessing. You don't care to be quite so predictable as the archetypal Capricorn would be, and there is a more idealistic quality here, or at least one that shows more. A greater number of friends than Capricorn usually keeps is likely, though less than the true Aquarian would gather. Few people doubt your sincerity, though by no means all of them understand what makes you tick. Unfortunately you are not in a position to help them out, because you are not too sure yourself. All the same, you muddle through and can be very capable when the mood takes you.

Being a natural traveller, you love to see new places and would be quite fascinated by cultures that are very different to your own. People with this combination are inclined to spend some time living abroad and may even settle there. You look out for the underdog and will always have time for a good cause, no matter what it takes to help. In romantic terms you are a reliable partner, though with a slightly wayward edge which, if anything, tends to make you even more attractive. Listen to your intuition, which is well honed and rarely lets you down. Generally speaking you are very popular.

THE MOON AND THE PART IT PLAYS IN YOUR LIFE

In astrology, the Moon is probably the single most important heavenly body after the Sun. Its unique position, as partner to the Earth on its journey around the solar system, means that the Moon appears to pass through the signs of the zodiac extremely quickly. The zodiac position of the Moon at the time of your birth plays a great part in personality and is especially significant in the build-up of your emotional nature.

Your Own Moon Sign

Discovering the position of the Moon at the time of your birth has always been notoriously difficult, because tracking the complex zodiac positions of the Moon is not easy. This process has been reduced to three simple stages with our Lunar Tables. A breakdown of the Moon's zodiac positions can be found from page 33 onwards, so that once you know what your Moon Sign is, you can see what part this plays in the overall build-up of your personal character.

If you follow the instructions on the next page, you will soon be able to work out exactly what zodiac sign the Moon occupied on the day that you were born. You can then go on to compare the reading for this position with those of your Sun sign and your Ascendant. It is partly the comparison between these three important positions that goes towards making you the unique individual you are.

HOW TO DISCOVER YOUR MOON SIGN

This is a three-stage process. You may need a pen and a piece of paper but if you follow the instructions below the process should only take a minute or so.

STAGE 1 First of all you need to know the Moon Age at the time of your birth. If you look at Moon Table 1, on page 33, you will find all the years between 1918 and 2016 down the left side. Find the year of your birth and then trace across to the right to the month of your birth. Where the two intersect you will find a number. This is the date of the New Moon in the month that you were born. You now need to count forward the number of days between the New Moon and your own birthday. For example, if the New Moon in the month of your birth was shown as being the 6th and you were born on the 20th, your Moon Age Day would be 14. If the New Moon in the month of your birth came after your birthday, you need to count forward from the New Moon in the previous month, which, if you were born in January, means you must look at December in the previous year. You cannot count from December in the year of your birth, as that month is *after* your birth. Whatever the result, jot this number down so that you do not forget it.

STAGE 2 Take a look at Moon Table 2 on page 34. Down the left hand column look for the date of your birth. Now trace across to the month of your birth. Where the two meet you will find a letter. Copy this letter down alongside your Moon Age Day.

STAGE 3 Moon Table 3 on page 34 will supply you with the zodiac sign the Moon occupied on the day of your birth. Look for your Moon Age Day down the left hand column and then for the letter you found in Stage 2. Where the two converge you will find a zodiac sign and this is the sign occupied by the Moon on the day that you were born.

Your Zodiac Moon Sign Explained

You will find a profile of all zodiac Moon Signs on pages 35 to 38, showing in yet another way how astrology can be used to explain the individual that you are. In each daily entry of the Astral Diary you can find the zodiac position of the Moon for every day of the year. This also allows you to discover your lunar birthdays. Since the Moon passes through all the signs of the zodiac in about a month, you can expect something like twelve lunar birthdays each year. At these times you are likely to be emotionally steady and able to make the sort of decisions that have real, lasting value.

MOON TABLE 1

YEAR	DEC	JAN	FEB	YEAR	DEC	JAN	FEB	YEAR	DEC	JAN	FEB
1918	2	12	11	1951	28	7	6	1984	22	3	1
1919	21	1/31	–	1952	17	26	25	1985	12	21	19
1920	10	20	19	1953	6	15	14	1986	1/30	10	9
1921	29	9	8	1954	25	5	3	1987	20	29	28
1922	18	27	26	1955	14	24	22	1988	9	19	17
1923	8	17	15	1956	2	13	11	1989	28	7	6
1924	26	6	5	1957	21	1/30	–	1990	17	26	25
1925	15	24	23	1958	10	19	18	1991	6	15	14
1926	5	14	12	1959	29	9	7	1992	24	4	3
1927	24	3	2	1960	18	27	26	1993	14	23	22
1928	12	21	19	1961	7	16	15	1994	2	11	10
1929	1/30	11	9	1962	26	6	5	1995	22	1/30	–
1930	19	29	28	1963	15	25	23	1996	10	20	18
1931	9	18	17	1964	4	14	13	1997	28	9	7
1932	27	7	6	1965	22	3	1	1998	18	27	26
1933	17	25	24	1966	12	21	19	1999	7	17	16
1934	6	15	14	1967	1/30	10	9	2000	26	6	4
1935	25	5	3	1968	20	29	28	2001	15	25	23
1936	13	24	22	1969	9	19	17	2002	4	13	12
1937	2	12	11	1970	28	7	6	2003	23	3	1
1938	21	1/31	–	1971	17	26	25	2004	11	21	20
1939	10	20	19	1972	6	15	14	2005	30	10	9
1940	28	9	8	1973	25	5	4	2006	20	29	28
1941	18	27	26	1974	14	24	22	2007	9	18	16
1942	8	16	15	1975	3	12	11	2008	27	8	6
1943	27	6	4	1976	21	1/31	29	2009	16	26	25
1944	15	25	24	1977	10	19	18	2010	6	15	14
1945	4	14	12	1978	29	9	7	2011	25	4	3
1946	23	3	2	1979	18	27	26	2012	12	23	22
1947	12	21	19	1980	7	16	15	2013	2	12	10
1948	1/30	11	9	1981	26	6	4	2014	2	1/31	–
1949	19	29	27	1982	15	25	23	2015	20	19	20
1950	9	18	16	1983	4	14	13	2016	29	9	8

33

TABLE 2

MOON TABLE 3

DAY	JAN	FEB	M/D	A	B	C	D	E	F	G
1	A	D	0	CP	AQ	AQ	AQ	PI	PI	PI
2	A	D	1	AQ	AQ	AQ	PI	PI	PI	AR
3	A	D	2	AQ	AQ	PI	PI	PI	AR	AR
4	A	D	3	AQ	PI	PI	PI	AR	AR	AR
5	A	D	4	PI	PI	AR	AR	AR	AR	TA
6	A	D	5	PI	AR	AR	AR	TA	TA	TA
7	A	D	6	AR	AR	AR	TA	TA	TA	GE
8	A	D	7	AR	AR	TA	TA	TA	GE	GE
9	A	D	8	AR	TA	TA	TA	GE	GE	GE
10	A	E	9	TA	TA	GE	GE	GE	CA	CA
11	B	E	10	TA	GE	GE	GE	CA	CA	CA
12	B	E	11	GE	GE	GE	CA	CA	CA	LE
13	B	E	12	GE	GE	CA	CA	CA	LE	LE
14	B	E	13	GE	CA	CA	LE	LE	LE	LE
15	B	E	14	CA	CA	LE	LE	LE	VI	VI
16	B	E	15	CA	LE	LE	LE	VI	VI	VI
17	B	E	16	LE	LE	LE	VI	VI	VI	LI
18	B	E	17	LE	LE	VI	VI	VI	LI	LI
19	B	E	18	LE	VI	VI	VI	LI	LI	LI
20	B	F	19	VI	VI	VI	LI	LI	LI	SC
21	C	F	20	VI	LI	LI	LI	SC	SC	SC
22	C	F	21	LI	LI	LI	SC	SC	SC	SA
23	C	F	22	LI	LI	SC	SC	SC	SA	SA
24	C	F	23	LI	SC	SC	SC	SA	SA	SA
25	C	F	24	SC	SC	SC	SA	SA	SA	CP
26	C	F	25	SC	SA	SA	SA	CP	CP	CP
27	C	F	26	SA	SA	SA	CP	CP	CP	AQ
28	C	F	27	SA	SA	CP	CP	AQ	AQ	AQ
29	C	F	28	SA	CP	CP	AQ	AQ	AQ	AQ
30	C	–	29	CP	CP	CP	AQ	AQ	AQ	PI
31	D	–								

AR = Aries, TA = Taurus, GE = Gemini, CA = Cancer, LE = Leo, VI = Virgo,
LI = Libra, SC = Scorpio, SA = Sagittarius, CP = Capricorn, AQ = Aquarius, PI = Pisces

MOON SIGNS

Moon in Aries

You have a strong imagination, courage, determination and a desire to do things in your own way and forge your own path through life.

Originality is a key attribute; you are seldom stuck for ideas although your mind is changeable and you should take the time to focus on individual tasks. Often quick tempered, you take orders from few people and live life at a fast pace. Avoid health problems by taking regular time out for rest and relaxation.

Emotionally, it is important that you talk to those you are closest to and work out your true feelings. Once you discover that people are there to help, there is less necessity for you to do everything yourself.

Moon in Taurus

The Moon in Taurus gives you a courteous and friendly manner, which means you are likely to have many friends.

The good things in life mean a lot to you, as Taurus is an Earth sign that delights in experiences which please the senses. Hence you are probably a lover of good food and drink, which may in turn mean you need to keep an eye on the bathroom scales, especially as looking good is also important to you.

Emotionally you are fairly stable and you stick by your own standards. Taureans do not respond well to change. Intuition also plays an important part in your life.

Moon in Gemini

You have a warm-hearted character, sympathetic and eager to help others. At times reserved, you can also be articulate and chatty: this is part of the paradox of Gemini, which always brings duplicity to someone's nature. You are interested in current affairs, have a good intellect, and are good company and likely to have many friends. Most of your friends have a high opinion of you and would be ready to defend you should the need arise. However, this is usually unnecessary, as you are quite capable of defending yourself in any verbal confrontation.

Travel is important to your inquisitive mind and you find intellectual stimulus in mixing with people from different cultures. You also gain much from reading, writing and the arts but you do need plenty of rest and relaxation in order to avoid fatigue.

Moon in Cancer

The Moon in Cancer at the time of birth is a fortunate position as Cancer is the Moon's natural home. This means that the qualities of compassion and understanding given by the Moon are especially enhanced in your nature, and you are friendly and sociable and cope well with emotional pressures. You cherish home and family life, and happily do the domestic tasks. Your surroundings are important to you and you hate squalor and filth. You are likely to have a love of music and poetry.

Your basic character, although at times changeable like the Moon itself, depends on symmetry. You aim to make your surroundings comfortable and harmonious, for yourself and those close to you.

Moon in Leo

The best qualities of the Moon and Leo come together to make you warm-hearted, fair, ambitious and self-confident. With good organisational abilities, you invariably rise to a position of responsibility in your chosen career. This is fortunate as you don't enjoy being an 'also-ran' and would rather be an important part of a small organisation than a menial in a large one.

You should be lucky in love, and happy, provided you put in the effort to make a comfortable home for yourself and those close to you. It is likely that you will have a love of pleasure, sport, music and literature. Life brings you many rewards, most of them as a direct result of your own efforts, although you may be luckier than average and ready to make the best of any situation.

Moon in Virgo

You are endowed with good mental abilities and a keen receptive memory, but you are never ostentatious or pretentious. Naturally quite reserved, you still have many friends. Marital relationships must be discussed carefully and worked at so that they remain harmonious, as personal attachments can be a problem if you do not give them your full attention.

Talented and persevering, you possess artistic qualities and are a good homemaker. Earning your honours through genuine merit, you work long and hard towards your objectives but show little pride in your achievements. Many short journeys will be undertaken in your life.

Moon in Libra

With the Moon in Libra you are naturally popular and make friends easily. People like you, probably more than you realise, you bring fun to a party and are a natural diplomat. For all its good points, Libra is not the most stable of astrological signs and, as a result, your emotions can be a little unstable too. Therefore, although the Moon in Libra is said to be good for love and marriage, your Sun sign and Rising sign will have an important effect on your emotional and loving qualities.

You must remember to relate to others in your decision-making. Co-operation is crucial because Libra represents the 'balance' of life that can only be achieved through harmonious relationships. Conformity is not easy for you because Libra, an Air sign, likes its independence.

Moon in Scorpio

Some people might call you pushy. In fact, all you really want to do is to live life to the full and protect yourself and your family from the pressures of life. Take care to avoid giving the impression of being sarcastic or impulsive and use your energies wisely and constructively.

You have great courage and you invariably achieve your goals by force of personality and sheer effort. You are fond of mystery and are good at predicting the outcome of situations and events. Travel experiences can be beneficial to you.

You may experience problems if you do not take time to examine your motives in a relationship, and also if you allow jealousy, always a feature of Scorpio, to cloud your judgement.

Moon in Sagittarius

The Moon in Sagittarius helps to make you a generous individual with humanitarian qualities and a kind heart. Restlessness may be intrinsic as your mind is seldom still. Perhaps because of this, you have a need for change that could lead you to several major moves during your adult life. You are not afraid to stand your ground when you know your judgement is right, you speak directly and have good intuition.

At work you are quick, efficient and versatile and so you make an ideal employee. You need work to be intellectually demanding and do not enjoy tedious routines.

In relationships, you anger quickly if faced with stupidity or deception, though you are just as quick to forgive and forget. Emotionally, there are times when your heart rules your head.

Moon in Capricorn

The Moon in Capricorn makes you popular and likely to come into the public eye in some way. The watery Moon is not entirely comfortable in the Earth sign of Capricorn and this may lead to some difficulties in the early years of life. An initial lack of creative ability and indecision must be overcome before the true qualities of patience and perseverance inherent in Capricorn can show through.

You have good administrative ability and are a capable worker, and if you are careful you can accumulate wealth. But you must be cautious and take professional advice in partnerships, as you are open to deception. You may be interested in social or welfare work, which suit your organisational skills and sympathy for others.

Moon in Aquarius

The Moon in Aquarius makes you an active and agreeable person with a friendly, easy-going nature. Sympathetic to the needs of others, you flourish in a laid-back atmosphere. You are broad-minded, fair and open to suggestion, although sometimes you have an unconventional quality which others can find hard to understand.

You are interested in the strange and curious, and in old articles and places. You enjoy trips to these places and gain much from them. Political, scientific and educational work interests you and you might choose a career in science or technology.

Money-wise, you make gains through innovation and concentration and Lunar Aquarians often tackle more than one job at a time. In love you are kind and honest.

Moon in Pisces

You have a kind, sympathetic nature, somewhat retiring at times, but you always take account of others' feelings and help when you can.

Personal relationships may be problematic, but as life goes on you can learn from your experiences and develop a better understanding of yourself and the world around you.

You have a fondness for travel, appreciate beauty and harmony and hate disorder and strife. You may be fond of literature and would make a good writer or speaker yourself. You have a creative imagination and may come across as an incurable romantic. You have strong intuition, maybe bordering on a mediumistic quality, which sets you apart from the mass. You may not be rich in cash terms, but your personal gifts are worth more than gold.

AQUARIUS IN LOVE

Discover how compatible in love you are with people from the same and other signs of the zodiac. Five stars equals a match made in heaven!

Aquarius meets Aquarius

This is a good match for several reasons. Most importantly, although it sounds arrogant, Aquarians like themselves. At its best, Aquarius is one of the fairest, most caring and genuinely pleasant zodiac signs and so it is only when faced by the difficulties created by others that it shows a less favourable side. Put two Aquarians together and voilà – instant success! Personal and family life should bring more joy. On the whole, a platform for adventure based on solid foundations. Star rating: *****

Aquarius meets Pisces

Zodiac signs that follow each other often have something in common, but this is not the case with Aquarius and Pisces. Both signs are deeply caring, but in different ways. Pisces is one of the deepest zodiac signs, and Aquarius simply isn't prepared to embark on the journey. Pisceans, meanwhile, would probably find Aquarians superficial and even flippant. On the positive side there is potential for a well-balanced relationship, but unless one party is untypical of their zodiac sign, it often doesn't get started. Star rating: **

Aquarius meets Aries

Aquarius is an Air sign, and Air and Fire often work well together, but not in the case of Aries and Aquarius. The average Aquarian lives in what the Ram sees as a fantasy world, so a meeting of minds is unlikely. Of course, the dominant side of Aries could be trained by the devil-may-care attitude of Aquarius. There are meeting points but they are difficult to establish. However, given sufficient time and an open mind on both sides, a degree of happiness is possible. Star rating: **

Aquarius meets Taurus

In any relationship of which Aquarius is a part, surprises abound. It is difficult for Taurus to understand the soul-searching, adventurous, changeable Aquarian, but on the positive side, the Bull is adaptable and can respond well to a dose of excitement. Aquarians are kind and react well to the same quality coming back at them. Both are friendly, capable of deep affection and basically creative. Unfortunately, Taurus simply doesn't know what makes Aquarius tick, which could lead to feelings of isolation, even if these don't always show on the surface. Star rating: **

Aquarius meets Gemini

Aquarius is commonly mistaken for a Water sign, but in fact it's ruled by the Air element, and this is the key to its compatibility with Gemini. Both signs mix freely in company, and each has an insatiable curiosity. There is plenty of action, lots of love, but very little rest, and so great potential for success if they don't wear each other out! Aquarius revels in its own eccentricity, and encourages Gemini to emulate this. Theirs will be an unconventional household, but almost everyone warms to this crazy and unpredictable couple. Star rating: *****

Aquarius meets Cancer

Cancer is often attracted to Aquarius, as Aquarius is automatically on the side of anyone who fancies it, so there is the potential for something good here. Cancer loves Aquarius' devil-may-care approach to life, but also recognises and seeks to strengthen the basic lack of self-confidence that all Air signs try so hard to keep secret. Both signs are natural travellers and are quite adventurous. Their family life could be unusual, but friends would recognise a caring, sharing household with many different interests shared by people genuinely in love. Star rating: ***

Aquarius meets Leo

The problem here is that Aquarius doesn't think in the general sense of the word, it knows. Leo, on the other hand, is more practical and relies more on logical reasoning, and consequently it doesn't understand Aquarius very well. Aquarians can also appear slightly frosty in their appreciation of others and this, too, will annoy Leo. This is a good match for a business partnership because Aquarius is astute, while Leo is brave, but personally the prognosis is less promising. Tolerance, understanding and forbearance are all needed to make this work. Star rating: **

Aquarius meets Virgo

Aquarius is a strange sign because no matter how well one knows it, it always manages to surprise. For this reason, against the odds, it's quite likely that Aquarius will form a sucessful relationship with Virgo. Aquarius is changeable, unpredictable and often quite odd, while Virgo is steady, a fuss-pot and very practical. Herein lies the key. What one sign needs, the other provides and that may be the surest recipe for success imaginable. On-lookers may not know why the couple are happy, but they will recognise that this is the case. Star rating: ****

Aquarius meets Libra

One of the best combinations imaginable, partly because both are Air signs and so share a common meeting point. But perhaps the more crucial factor is that both signs respect each other. Aquarius loves life and originality, and is quite intellectual. Libra is similar, but more balanced and rather less eccentric. A visit to this couple's house would be entertaining and full of zany wit, activity and excitement. Both are keen to travel and may prefer to 'find themselves' before taking on too many domestic responsibilities. Star rating: *****

Aquarius meets Scorpio

This is a promising and practical combination. Scorpio responds well to Aquarius' persistent exploration of its deep nature and so this generally shy sign becomes lighter, brighter and more inspirational. Meanwhile, Aquarians are rarely as sure of themselves as they like to appear and are reassured by Scorpio's constant, steady and determined support. Both signs want to be kind to each other, which is a good starting point to a relationship that should be warm most of the time and extremely hot occasionally. Star rating: ****

Aquarius meets Sagittarius

Both Sagittarius and Aquarius are into mind games, which may lead to something of an intellectual competition. If one side is happy to be 'bamboozled' it won't be a problem, but it is more likely that the relationship will turn into a competition, which won't auger well for its long-term future. However, on the plus side, both signs are adventurous and sociable, so as long as there is always something new and interesting to do, the match could turn out very well. Star rating: **

Aquarius meets Capricorn

Probably one of the least likely combinations, as Capricorn and Aquarius are unlikely to choose each other in the first place, unless one side is quite untypical of their sign. Capricorn approaches things in a practical way and likes to get things done, while Aquarius works almost exclusively for the moment and relies heavily on intuition. Their attitudes to romance are also diametrically opposed: Aquarius' moods tend to swing from red hot to ice cold in a minute, which is alien to steady Capricorn. Star rating: **

VENUS:
THE PLANET OF LOVE

If you look up at the sky around sunset or sunrise you will often see Venus in close attendance to the Sun. It is arguably one of the most beautiful sights of all and there is little wonder that historically it became associated with the goddess of love. But although Venus does play an important part in the way you view love and in the way others see you romantically, this is only one of the spheres of influence that it enjoys in your overall character.

Venus has a part to play in the more cultured side of your life and has much to do with your appreciation of art, literature, music and general creativity. Even the way you look is responsive to the part of the zodiac that Venus occupied at the start of your life, though this fact is also down to your Sun sign and Ascending sign. If, at the time you were born, Venus occupied one of the more gregarious zodiac signs, you will be more likely to wear your heart on your sleeve, as well as to be more attracted to entertainment, social gatherings and good company. If on the other hand Venus occupied a quiet zodiac sign at the time of your birth, you would tend to be more retiring and less willing to shine in public situations.

It's good to know what part the planet Venus plays in your life for it can have a great bearing on the way you appear to the rest of the world and since we all have to mix with others, you can learn to make the very best of what Venus has to offer you.

One of the great complications in the past has always been trying to establish exactly what zodiac position Venus enjoyed when you were born because the planet is notoriously difficult to track. However, we have solved that problem by creating a table that is exclusive to your Sun sign, which you will find on the following page.

Establishing your Venus sign could not be easier. Just look up the year of your birth on the following page and you will see a sign of the zodiac. This was the sign that Venus occupied in the period covered by your sign in that year. If Venus occupied more than one sign during the period, this is indicated by the date on which the sign changed, and the name of the new sign. For instance, if you were born in 1945, Venus was in Pisces until the 12th February, after which time it was in Aries. If you were born before 12th February your Venus sign is Pisces, if you were born on or after 12th February, your Venus sign is Aries. Once you have established the position of Venus at the time of your birth, you can then look in the pages which follow to see how this has a bearing on your life as a whole.

1918 AQUARIUS
1919 AQUARIUS / 3.2 PISCES
1920 SAGITTARIUS / 30.1 CAPRICORN
1921 PISCES / 15.2 ARIES
1922 CAPRICORN / 25.1 AQUARIUS /
   18.2 PISCES
1923 SAGITTARIUS / 7.2 CAPRICORN
1924 PISCES / 13.2 ARIES
1925 CAPRICORN / 9.2 AQUARIUS
1926 AQUARIUS
1927 AQUARIUS / 2.2 PISCES
1928 SAGITTARIUS / 29.1 CAPRICORN
1929 PISCES / 14.2 ARIES
1930CAPRICORN / 25.1 AQUARIUS /
   18.2 PISCES
1931 SAGITTARIUS / 6.2 CAPRICORN
1932 PISCES / 13.2 ARIES
1933 CAPRICORN / 8.2 AQUARIUS
1934 AQUARIUS
1935 AQUARIUS / 2.2 PISCES
1936 SAGITTARIUS / 29.1 CAPRICORN
1937 PISCES / 13.2 ARIES
1938 CAPRICORN / 24.1 AQUARIUS /
   17.2 PISCES
1939 SAGITTARIUS / 6.2 CAPRICORN
1940 PISCES / 12.2 ARIES
1941 CAPRICORN / 8.2 AQUARIUS
1942 AQUARIUS
1943 AQUARIUS / 1.2 PISCES
1944 SAGITTARIUS / 28.1 CAPRICORN
1945 PISCES / 12.2 ARIES
1946 CAPRICORN / 24.1 AQUARIUS /
   17.2 PISCES
1947 SAGITTARIUS / 6.2 CAPRICORN
1948 PISCES / 12.2 ARIES
1949 CAPRICORN / 7.2 AQUARIUS
1950 AQUARIUS
1951 AQUARIUS / 1.2 PISCES
1952 SAGITTARIUS / 27.1 CAPRICORN
1953 PISCES / 11.2 ARIES
1954 CAPRICORN / 23.1 AQUARIUS /
   16.2 PISCES
1955 SAGITTARIUS / 6.2 CAPRICORN
1956 PISCES / 11.2 ARIES
1957 CAPRICORN / 7.2 AQUARIUS
1958 AQUARIUS
1959 AQUARIUS / 31.1 PISCES
1960 SAGITTARIUS / 27.1 CAPRICORN
1961 PISCES / 9.2 ARIES
1962 CAPRICORN / 23.1 AQUARIUS /
   15.2 PISCES
1963 SAGITTARIUS / 6.2 CAPRICORN
1964 PISCES / 11.2 ARIES
1965 CAPRICORN / 6.2 AQUARIUS

1966 AQUARIUS
1967 AQUARIUS / 30.1 PISCES
1968 SAGITTARIUS / 26.1 CAPRICORN
1969 PISCES / 7.2 ARIES
1970 CAPRICORN / 22.1 AQUARIUS /
   15.2 PISCES
1971 SAGITTARIUS / 5.2 CAPRICORN
1972 PISCES / 10.2 ARIES
1973 CAPRICORN / 5.2 AQUARIUS
1974 AQUARIUS / 7.2 CAPRICORN
1975 AQUARIUS / 30.1 PISCES
1976 SAGITTARIUS / 26.1 CAPRICORN
1977 PISCES / 5.2 ARIES
1978 CAPRICORN / 22.1 AQUARIUS /
   14.2 PISCES
1979 SAGITTARIUS / 5.2 CAPRICORN
1980 PISCES / 10.2 ARIES
1981 CAPRICORN / 5.2 AQUARIUS
1982 AQUARIUS / 29.1 CAPRICORN
1983 AQUARIUS / 29.1 PISCES
1984 SAGITTARIUS / 25.1 CAPRICORN
1985 PISCES / 5.2 ARIES
1986 AQUARIUS / 14.2 PISCES
1987 SAGITTARIUS / 5.2 CAPRICORN
1988 PISCES / 9.2 ARIES
1989 CAPRICORN / 4.2 AQUARIUS
1990 AQUARIUS / 23.1 CAPRICORN
1991 AQUARIUS / 29.1 PISCES
1992 SAGITTARIUS / 25.1 CAPRICORN
1993 PISCES / 4.2 ARIES
1994 AQUARIUS / 13.2 PISCES
1995 SAGITTARIUS / 5.2 CAPRICORN
1996 PISCES / 9.2 ARIES
1997 CAPRICORN / 4.2 AQUARIUS
1998 AQUARIUS / 23.1 CAPRICORN
1999 AQUARIUS / 29.1 PISCES
2000 SAGITTARIUS / 25.1 CAPRICORN
2001 PISCES / 4.2 ARIES
2002 AQUARIUS / 13.2 PISCES
2003 SAGITTARIUS
2004 PISCES / 9.2 AQUARIUS
2005 CAPRICORN / 6.2 AQUARIUS
2006 AQUARIUS / 14.01 CAPRICORN
2007 AQUARIUS / 19.01 PISCES
2008 SAGITTARIUS / 25.1 CAPRICORN
2009 PISCES / 4.2 ARIES
2010 AQUARIUS / 12.2 PISCES
2011 SAGITTARIUS
2012 PISCES / 9.2 AQUARIUS
2013 CAPRICORN / 6.2 AQUARIUS
2014 CAPRICORN / 6.2 AQUARIUS
2015 AQUARIUS / 29.1 PISCES
2016 SAGITTARIUS / 24.1 AQUARIUS

VENUS THROUGH THE ZODIAC SIGNS

Venus in Aries

Amongst other things, the position of Venus in Aries indicates a fondness for travel, music and all creative pursuits. Your nature tends to be affectionate and you try not to create confusion or difficulty for others if it can be avoided. Many people with this planetary position have a great love of the theatre, and mental stimulation is of the greatest importance. Early romantic attachments are common with Venus in Aries, so it is very important to establish a genuine sense of romantic continuity. Early marriage is not recommended, especially if it is based on sympathy. You may give your heart a little too readily on occasions.

Venus in Taurus

You are capable of very deep feelings and your emotions tend to last for a very long time. This makes you a trusting partner and lover, whose constancy is second to none. In life you are precise and careful and always try to do things the right way. Although this means an ordered life, which you are comfortable with, it can also lead you to be rather too fussy for your own good. Despite your pleasant nature, you are very fixed in your opinions and quite able to speak your mind. Others are attracted to you and historical astrologers always quoted this position of Venus as being very fortunate in terms of marriage. However, if you find yourself involved in a failed relationship, it could take you a long time to trust again.

Venus in Gemini

As with all associations related to Gemini, you tend to be quite versatile, anxious for change and intelligent in your dealings with the world at large. You may gain money from more than one source but you are equally good at spending it. There is an inference here that you are a good communicator, either in the written or the spoken word, and you love to be in the company of interesting people. Always on the look-out for culture, you may also be very fond of music, and love to indulge the curious and cultured side of your nature. In romance you tend to have more than one relationship and could find yourself associated with someone who has previously been a friend or even a distant relative.

Venus in Cancer

You often stay close to home because you are very fond of family and enjoy many of your most treasured moments when you are with those you love. Being naturally sympathetic, you will always do anything you can to support those around you, even people you hardly know at all. This charitable side of your nature is your most noticeable trait and is one of the reasons why others are naturally so fond of you. Being receptive and in some cases even psychic, you can see through to the soul of most of those with whom you come into contact. You may not commence too many romantic attachments but when you do give your heart, it tends to be unconditionally.

Venus in Leo

It must become quickly obvious to almost anyone you meet that you are kind, sympathetic and yet determined enough to stand up for anyone or anything that is truly important to you. Bright and sunny, you warm the world with your natural enthusiasm and would rarely do anything to hurt those around you, or at least not intentionally. In romance you are ardent and sincere, though some may find your style just a little overpowering. Gains come through your contacts with other people and this could be especially true with regard to romance, for love and money often come hand in hand for those who were born with Venus in Leo. People claim to understand you, though you are more complex than you seem.

Venus in Virgo

Your nature could well be fairly quiet no matter what your Sun sign might be, though this fact often manifests itself as an inner peace and does not prevent you from being basically sociable. Some delays and even the odd disappointment in love cannot be ruled out with this planetary position, though it's a fact that you will usually find the happiness you look for in the end. Catapulting yourself into romantic entanglements that you know to be rather ill-advised is not sensible, and it would be better to wait before you commit yourself exclusively to any one person. It is the essence of your nature to serve the world at large and through doing so it is possible that you will attract money at some stage in your life.

Venus in Libra

Venus is very comfortable in Libra and bestows upon those people who have this planetary position a particular sort of kindness that is easy to recognise. This is a very good position for all sorts of friendships and also for romantic attachments that usually bring much joy into your life. Few individuals with Venus in Libra would avoid marriage and since you are capable of great depths of love, it is likely that you will find a contented personal life. You like to mix with people of integrity and intelligence but don't take kindly to scruffy surroundings or work that means getting your hands too dirty. Careful speculation, good business dealings and money through marriage all seem fairly likely.

Venus in Scorpio

You are quite open and tend to spend money quite freely, even on those occasions when you don't have very much. Although your intentions are always good, there are times when you get yourself in to the odd scrape and this can be particularly true when it comes to romance, which you may come to late or from a rather unexpected direction. Certainly you have the power to be happy and to make others contented on the way, but you find the odd stumbling block on your journey through life and it could seem that you will have to work harder than those around you. As a result of this, you gain a much deeper understanding of the true value of personal happiness than many people ever do, and are likely to achieve true contentment in the end.

Venus in Sagittarius

You are lighthearted, cheerful and always able to see the funny side of any situation. These facts enhance your popularity. You should never have to look too far to find romantic interest in your life, though it is just possible that you might be too willing to commit yourself before you are certain that someone is right for you. Part of the problem here extends to other areas of life too. The fact is that you like variety in everything and so can tire of situations that fail to offer it. All the same, if you choose wisely and learn to understand your restless side, then great happiness can be yours.

Venus in Capricorn

The most notable trait that comes from Venus in this position is that it makes you trustworthy and able to take on all sorts of responsibilities in life. People are instinctively fond of you and love you all the more because you are always ready to help those who are in any form of need. Social and business popularity can be yours and there is a magnetic quality to your nature that is particularly attractive in a romantic sense. Anyone who wants a partner for a lover, a spouse and a good friend too would almost certainly look in your direction. Constancy is the hallmark of your nature and unfaithfulness goes right against the grain. You might sometimes be a little too trusting.

Venus in Aquarius

This location of Venus offers a fondness for travel and a desire to try out something new at every possible opportunity. You are extremely easy to get along with and tend to have many friends from varied backgrounds, classes and inclinations. You like to live a distinct sort of life and gain a great deal from moving about, both in a career sense and with regard to your home. It is not out of the question that you could form a romantic attachment to someone who comes from far away or be attracted to a person of a distinctly artistic and original nature. What you cannot stand is jealousy, for you have friends of both sexes and would want to keep things that way.

Venus in Pisces

The first thing people tend to notice about you is your wonderful, warm smile. Being very charitable by nature you will do anything to help others, even if you don't know them well. Much of your life may be spent sorting out situations for other people, but it is very important to feel that you are living for yourself too. In the main, you remain cheerful, and tend to be quite attractive to others. Where romantic attachments are concerned, you could be drawn to people who are significantly older or younger than yourself or to someone with a unique career or point of view. It might be best for you to avoid marrying whilst you are still very young.

AQUARIUS:
2015 DIARY PAGES

October

2015

1 THURSDAY ☿ *Moon Age Day 18 Moon Sign Taurus*

Your major new focus is now on leisure and romantic matters. With everything working generally well you should be able to see quite easily how attractive you are to others. There are distinct gains to be made at this time from simply being what you naturally are. Personalities abound, both at work and socially.

2 FRIDAY ☿ *Moon Age Day 19 Moon Sign Gemini*

This is a favourable time where your finances are concerned. This would be a good time to look at money and to work out how best to plan for the future. At the same time, there is a strong social quality to the day and you don't have any trouble in mixing business with pleasure.

3 SATURDAY ☿ *Moon Age Day 20 Moon Sign Gemini*

Although part of you is anxious to make progress, there are aspects of your mind that are restricted and far from forward-looking. Take on board the needs of those close to you and, if at all possible, enjoy a family day. Don't get involved in discussions that could easily lead to arguments.

4 SUNDAY ☿ *Moon Age Day 21 Moon Sign Gemini*

You should find that any work in progress at the moment is both rewarding and materially satisfying. There are positive signs around movement on most fronts. Be aware that it might sometimes be difficult to understand the motivations of close relatives and a little probing could be necessary.

5 MONDAY   ☿   *Moon Age Day 22 Moon Sign Cancer*

There ought to be plenty of ways you can feed your ego at the moment. After all, it isn't the voracious monster that is the case with some zodiac signs. Nevertheless, you need to be preened now and again and to know how important you are to those around you. Fishing for compliments might bring a bigger than expected catch today.

6 TUESDAY   ☿   *Moon Age Day 23 Moon Sign Cancer*

If you have wanted to make any sort of fresh start, or improvements and changes to your home, this is probably the best time to get cracking. Enlist the support of family members and plan what you are going to do. It's really a case of taking the bull by the horns today.

7 WEDNESDAY   ☿   *Moon Age Day 24 Moon Sign Leo*

You may have to cut your losses regarding a present project in order to make the very best of what lies in store for later. Arrangements for later should be made today, especially if you are looking forward to an important social gathering of some sort. Your partner might seem out of sorts today.

8 THURSDAY   ☿   *Moon Age Day 25 Moon Sign Leo*

Don't expect life to follow a particularly smooth course today. The 'lunar low' is inclined to bring complications and it can prevent you from following through in projects that are presently quite important to you. Although you are quite sporting at the moment, it will be harder to get past the winning post first.

9 FRIDAY   ☿   *Moon Age Day 26 Moon Sign Virgo*

This is probably the best day of the month in which to express your love for someone very special indeed. Although you might be committed to work, you are also entering a period in which a sense of personal freedom is especially important. As a result, you need to try to arrange some sort of break later in the day.

10 SATURDAY   ☿   *Moon Age Day 27 Moon Sign Virgo*

With a more competitive streak now firmly on display, you will want to push forward on all fronts. This might not be especially easy and you will need to use extra effort to get ahead of some of the small difficulties that surround you. Acting on impulse comes as second nature.

11 SUNDAY   ☿   *Moon Age Day 28 Moon Sign Virgo*

You are willing to work hard and to do whatever it takes to get to your chosen destination. Don't get bogged down with details today, but instead stick to the main themes of life. It's the big picture that counts. By the evening, you will probably be quite happy to relax in the bosom of your family.

12 MONDAY   *Moon Age Day 29 Moon Sign Libra*

So far this month, you have made fairly good progress in material matters and now comes a time when it seems important to consolidate your efforts. Some ingenuity is obvious and you can be fairly definite in your actions. That might not seem like much, but it's very important to Aquarius.

13 TUESDAY   *Moon Age Day 0 Moon Sign Libra*

Check up on financial management today, because it's possible that you haven't been taking as much notice of your bank account as you should have. Don't worry: things are not likely to be as bad as you might first think. It would be fair to say that you are rather more pessimistic than usual.

14 WEDNESDAY   *Moon Age Day 1 Moon Sign Scorpio*

A period of significant progress is still evident, particularly with regard to your personal plans. Specialist help is available when you need it the most and you shouldn't have to look far in order to discover your great potential. Popularity is also high, which is always encouraging.

15 THURSDAY   *Moon Age Day 2 Moon Sign Scorpio*

In-depth discussions will probably take place today, but how much they are worth remains to be seen. In the main, you will want to spend at least short periods of time on your own or in the company of those you love and trust. By tomorrow, any temporary negative trends will be out of the way, so be patient.

16 FRIDAY   *Moon Age Day 3 Moon Sign Scorpio*

New information is likely to put you fully in the picture today, which will enable you to make progress in many different areas of your life. However, much of what stands around you is only potential and the outcome depends on your own efforts. Fortunately, there are some very supportive trends around right now.

17 SATURDAY   *Moon Age Day 4 Moon Sign Sagittarius*

There are some important things to do today, but few of them will turn out to be quite as simple as you might wish. Still, it is possible to apply a little concentration, just as long as you don't try to tackle too many tasks at the same time. With communication well starred, later in the day you might get a call you have been expecting for a while.

18 SUNDAY   *Moon Age Day 5 Moon Sign Sagittarius*

Today marks a time when you will be busy enough, but there ought to be moments for contemplation and for getting your head round problems that might have been with you for a while. Even casual conversations can offer significant clues about the best way forward in a practical sense. Meanwhile, you could find love to be inviting.

19 MONDAY   *Moon Age Day 6 Moon Sign Capricorn*

Work and career issues tend to keep you on the go now, and there is hardly likely to be enough time to do everything that you would wish. Keep an open mind when it comes to changes that are now on the cards and don't spend too much time worrying about what might happen. Most decisions will be yours to make.

20 TUESDAY   *Moon Age Day 7   Moon Sign Capricorn*

Along comes a flurry of social invitations and some of these will detract from your ability to concentrate on strictly practical matters when they matter the most. Never mind. It's an interesting period all the same and, being an Aquarian, you need the stimulus that comes from interacting with others.

21 WEDNESDAY   *Moon Age Day 8   Moon Sign Capricorn*

You have lots to do at the moment, but you might not be feeling all that bright. The Moon is in your solar twelfth house, which more or less demands at least short periods of meditation and thought. Put a few routines on the back burner and try to enjoy a relaxing sort of evening, at least.

22 THURSDAY   *Moon Age Day 9   Moon Sign Aquarius*

Positive thinking really does pay off well today. The 'lunar high' brings much-needed light and energy into your life, so virtually nothing is beyond your capabilities. Something that has been at the back of your mind and that has been troubling you of late can now be addressed and settled.

23 FRIDAY   *Moon Age Day 10   Moon Sign Aquarius*

An element of serendipity shows itself in your life at the moment. There could well be significant gains, even when you are not particularly trying. The world and his dog are willing to help you towards your objectives and there is no doubt at all that a little cheek goes a very long way.

24 SATURDAY   *Moon Age Day 11   Moon Sign Pisces*

You will now get more involved in domestic matters than has been possible for a week or so. Your mind turns towards the demands that loved ones make of you and much of your spare time is being used to make others feel more secure. Leave a few moments just for yourself and take some time out to meditate.

25 SUNDAY *Moon Age Day 12 Moon Sign Pisces*

There are signs that you are going through a fairly stable period where money matters are concerned, so you should be able to deal with financial matters in a positive way. The real prospects for gain seem to be at work and you have all it takes to make a good impression. That might not be much use if you are not a weekend worker.

26 MONDAY *Moon Age Day 13 Moon Sign Aries*

Your powers of persuasion are well starred at the moment, so you should have very little difficulty in getting others to follow your lead. This can be especially useful at work, where you are probably in the running for advancement of some sort. The world tends to be the way you make it right now, so think big.

27 TUESDAY *Moon Age Day 14 Moon Sign Aries*

Things remain good for you in a social sense now and getting on with people who were difficult a few days ago should be quite easy. Routines could be tiresome, which is exactly why you tend to ignore them if you can. You are on top form artistically and this could be a good time for planning changes at home.

28 WEDNESDAY *Moon Age Day 15 Moon Sign Taurus*

There is one specific piece of advice that really matters today: get organised. You really do need to be on the ball and to prove to everyone around you that you know what you are doing and that you have a plan. Once people see that you are not simply bluffing your way through situations, co-operation is assured.

29 THURSDAY *Moon Age Day 16 Moon Sign Taurus*

It won't always be easy today to see a point of view that you just don't understand, but it's only a matter of time before explanations are available. It is probable that there are some events taking place right now to which you cannot be a party to for the moment. Try to curb your natural curiosity a little.

30 FRIDAY
Moon Age Day 17 Moon Sign Gemini

Intimate relationships bring promising moments and should help the working week to end in a very favourable way. You have what it takes to win hearts, so if there is someone around you have been wishing to sweep off their feet it seems as though this would be a good time to give it a go.

31 SATURDAY
Moon Age Day 18 Moon Sign Gemini

The prospect of new friendships on the horizon is welcome at a time when present attachments might be in doubt. Don't be too worried if you can't get family members to follow your instructions today. Leave them to their own devices and get on with what is important to you now.

November 2015

1 SUNDAY
Moon Age Day 19 Moon Sign Cancer

You need to keep things varied today. The more change and diversity you get into your life, the better you are going to enjoy what this Sunday has to offer. Leave all serious issues until another day and show how spontaneous you can be. You can also gain by simply being in the right place at the best time.

2 MONDAY
Moon Age Day 20 Moon Sign Cancer

You might be slightly better off from a financial point of view than you had been expecting. It could be that you have miscalculated or maybe you have simply been working much harder of late. In business, this could turn out to be a good time for important decisions that have been delayed.

3 TUESDAY
Moon Age Day 21 Moon Sign Leo

This is a time best used as a rest period between more active interludes. If you insist on knocking your head against a brick wall, all that results is a headache. Rather than struggling on when you know the trends are not good, take some time out to look and listen. The exercise is well worthwhile.

4 WEDNESDAY
Moon Age Day 22 Moon Sign Leo

Another slightly quieter day during which you continue to take stock. It might seem that the world is not an especially friendly place, but that is only because you are more inclined than usual to look on the black side. At least one person proves how concerned he or she is about you.

5 THURSDAY
Moon Age Day 23 Moon Sign Leo

You will probably desire a little privacy at the moment, but this is not a situation that is likely to last very long. On the contrary, by tomorrow you will be right on the ball, so it would be sensible to get yourself ready for what lies ahead. Friends appear to be extra sensitive today.

6 FRIDAY
Moon Age Day 24 Moon Sign Virgo

There is still a busy feel to life, so much so that paying the attention you should to others may now be quite difficult. Keep as focused as possible, because there are many potential distractions and one or two could lead you in entirely the wrong direction. Don't be frightened of your own success if it materialises.

7 SATURDAY
Moon Age Day 25 Moon Sign Virgo

Getting your own way should not be all that difficult. Rather than simply settling for what seems like a compromise, push forward and go for gold. Routines can be a bit of a drag and there is every reason to believe you will be ringing the changes in both your working life and at home.

8 SUNDAY
Moon Age Day 26 Moon Sign Libra

With great willpower and self-confidence, you are now inclined to take life by the scruff of the neck and to shake it into the shape you wish. This might mean having to be slightly less considerate of the needs of others, but even Aquarius has to be just a little selfish once in a while.

9 MONDAY
Moon Age Day 27 Moon Sign Libra

Practical matters should progress well at the beginning of this week and you are pretty much committed to your work. If you are engaged in full-time education, you need to study harder than ever now. It isn't so much what you know that counts, but rather the way you put it across.

10 TUESDAY
Moon Age Day 28 Moon Sign Libra

You have a natural instinct for analysing all situations today and tend to reach some quite radical conclusions as a result. Not everyone is what they appear to be, something you realise now with startling clarity. Keep your considered opinions to yourself for just a day or two longer.

11 WEDNESDAY
Moon Age Day 29 Moon Sign Scorpio

You will do your very best to arrive at decisions that suit the greatest number of people today, but you have to bear in mind that you can rarely (if ever) please everyone. In the main, you are in harmony with your surroundings and won't be too anxious to upset any applecart, be it social or personal.

12 THURSDAY
Moon Age Day 0 Moon Sign Scorpio

In some circles, a few people will consider your present style to be too impulsive, but they are almost certain to be attracted to you all the same. A positive attitude on your part, coupled with an understanding of necessary actions, will certainly pay dividends. You won't be keen to stand in any queue at the moment.

13 FRIDAY
Moon Age Day 1 Moon Sign Sagittarius

Avoid being too impulsive when you know that a more measured approach would please others more. You are always good at weighing up those around you and this ability is stronger than ever now. Use it to your advantage, even if this means a little manipulation on your part.

14 SATURDAY
Moon Age Day 2 Moon Sign Sagittarius

The planetary emphasis is now on finances and the sense of personal security that seems to be so important to you. At the same time, you are showing a very original streak in your social life and should be mixing with individuals who have not formed a part of your immediate circle before.

15 SUNDAY
Moon Age Day 3 Moon Sign Sagittarius

Now you are intent on helping others at a practical level. Little things you do for them have big consequences later on and what you excel at the most is inspiring confidence. This is a Sunday that gets you noticed by those around you and during which you don't tend to procrastinate at all.

16 MONDAY
Moon Age Day 4 Moon Sign Capricorn

There could be just a little luck in the financial sphere around this time and you need to be on the ball when it comes to any sort of deal that is in the offing. Look out for the odd practical mishap that could result from you being a little clumsier than usual.

17 TUESDAY
Moon Age Day 5 Moon Sign Capricorn

Take a little trip and make some changes to the routines of your life, if you can. It would be all too easy to become bored with things at the moment and in order to avoid this happening you may have to put in a little extra effort. You presently show great consideration for family members.

18 WEDNESDAY
Moon Age Day 6 Moon Sign Aquarius

This should turn out to be a day that is especially fulfilling. Whatever you decide to do is accomplished with little effort and you should keep a smile on your face for most of the time. Fresh starts are indicated and these are just as likely in your home life as they are at work.

19 THURSDAY
Moon Age Day 7 Moon Sign Aquarius

Today is a high spot and a time when Lady Luck is with you. Thoughts of comfort and security are out of the window, because you are more than willing to take a chance and to push things further than usual. Personal attachments are favoured today.

20 FRIDAY
Moon Age Day 8 Moon Sign Pisces

You remain basically optimistic and committed to the future, though there could be the odd setback today. You will need to keep your wits about you if you don't want to start again at the beginning with some specific projects. It may be best to settle for a fairly steady day – but that might be too much to expect.

21 SATURDAY
Moon Age Day 9 Moon Sign Pisces

You are likely to be out and about more than ever today and the weekend offers much to those Aquarians who are genuinely willing to put themselves out. There isn't any use in waiting around for anyone else to make the arrangements. Although you will have to work hard to get others involved, the effort will be more than worthwhile.

22 SUNDAY
Moon Age Day 10 Moon Sign Aries

Learning new things can be a great deal of fun this Sunday and you launch yourself into projects with a great deal of enthusiasm. Certain people could prove to be difficult, so you will have to show great diplomacy if you are to avoid getting into some sort of disagreement or even a downright row.

23 MONDAY
Moon Age Day 11 Moon Sign Aries

Communication with others is enlivening and even exciting at the start of this new working week. You tend to be acting on impulse for much of the time, but this is so much a part of your basic nature that it isn't any sort of problem. Listen to the ideas of a colleague because they could suit you, too.

24 TUESDAY
Moon Age Day 12 Moon Sign Taurus

It is likely that you will be somewhat argumentative today and you need to curb this tendency if you want to avoid falling out with someone who is in a position to do you a great deal of good. Count to ten before you react and keep your cool, even when you are faced with people you see as being deliberately stupid.

25 WEDNESDAY   *Moon Age Day 13 Moon Sign Taurus*

This should prove to be one of the better days of the month during which to enjoy friendship and the simple things of life. If you feel a bit lacklustre, a temporary change of scene could do the trick. When a particular task gets boring or frustrating, put it aside for a while.

26 THURSDAY   *Moon Age Day 14 Moon Sign Gemini*

Family and domestic situations are likely to prevail today. Get together with your loved ones and make some plans for the future. It is likely that one of your chief concerns will be Christmas, which is only a month away. When it comes to domestic chores, do your best to be inventive and to change the order in which you do things.

27 FRIDAY   *Moon Age Day 15 Moon Sign Gemini*

Look towards a relaxing and interesting sort of day, but also a time during which you will have to think deeply about an issue that has been on your mind for a while. You are quite chilled-out at present, so you can deal with situations better and can find answers that have eluded you for a few weeks or even months.

28 SATURDAY   *Moon Age Day 16 Moon Sign Cancer*

Beware of situations that could take you by surprise. Most of these are likely to be positive in nature and it appears that you are about to reap the benefits of efforts you have put in previously. The warmest and most endearing qualities of your nature are on display this weekend.

29 SUNDAY   *Moon Age Day 17 Moon Sign Cancer*

You need to widen your horizons whenever you can. Don't just look at the possible, but also stretch yourself whenever you can. The tendency to feel bored by life is hovering around and you need to do everything you can to counteract this trend. Seek out interesting people and new situations.

30 MONDAY
Moon Age Day 18 Moon Sign Cancer

Take every possible opportunity to get away from the ordinary in life. Winter is here and things can start to look very grey and uninspiring unless you put in that extra bit of effort. Aquarius has the power to lift its own spirits and those of everyone with whom it comes into contact.

2015

1 TUESDAY
Moon Age Day 19 Moon Sign Leo

You must guard against negative thinking. It would be a mistake to let any vital information pass you by, so it is important to keep looking and listening. Someone is in a very good position to offer you invaluable assistance, but that isn't much use if you fail to notice the fact.

2 WEDNESDAY
Moon Age Day 20 Moon Sign Leo

Perhaps it is now time to let go of the reins for a few hours and to allow others to do the driving. The 'lunar low' is inclined to make you feel less positive and also saps your strength significantly. It isn't that anything specific is likely to go wrong, merely that you are not quite as positive as you have been of late.

3 THURSDAY
Moon Age Day 21 Moon Sign Virgo

The potential for success exists in all matters to do with communication. You know what to say and have the knowing knack of getting others to do your bidding. Using a mixture of psychology and simple logic, you are even able to wind superiors and colleagues around your little finger.

4 FRIDAY
Moon Age Day 22 Moon Sign Virgo

You could do with a slightly firmer approach to family or domestic matters, maybe because those around you are allowing things to drift. Taking the initiative comes as second nature under present planetary trends, even if that means you rub someone up the wrong way as a result.

5 SATURDAY
Moon Age Day 23   Moon Sign Libra

News that is significant and even heart-warming seems to be coming your way at any time now. There is a practical element to everything you do, but it is quite feasible to mix business with pleasure. Romance shines out in the evening and social trends are gradually looking better.

6 SUNDAY
Moon Age Day 24   Moon Sign Libra

Your natural generosity will attract a good deal of attention, but you need to keep your eye on expenditure. It's all very well splashing money about, but you are going to need quite a lot before this month is out. Make sure the assistance you give is in kind and not in cash.

7 MONDAY
Moon Age Day 25   Moon Sign Libra

There is likely to be a restlessness about you at the start of this working week and you certainly will not take kindly to others telling you what you should be doing. You know your own routines best and will be anxious to follow your own ideas, especially when it comes to work.

8 TUESDAY
Moon Age Day 26   Moon Sign Scorpio

Persuasive and communicative, you must guard against negative thinking, but you do have a great set of incentives and should find it child's play to get others to follow your lead. As the day goes on, you discover more and more that pleases you, and tend to be quite attractive to those around you.

9 WEDNESDAY
Moon Age Day 27   Moon Sign Scorpio

Though the obligations you feel to others might be slightly frustrating today, you do need to bear them in mind. They say that no person is an island, and this is particularly true in your case at the moment. If you alienate yourself from those who have it in their power to help you, the results could be tiresome.

10 THURSDAY   *Moon Age Day 28 Moon Sign Sagittarius*

Although personal relationships might be rather downbeat for now, you need to take your joys where you can find them. Today that means friendship and the support that particular individuals are offering. In a practical sense, it would be best not to take anything for granted, especially at work.

11 FRIDAY   *Moon Age Day 0 Moon Sign Sagittarius*

Friday should bring a period of swifter progress. If you put on a spurt, you can steal a march on someone who has been beating you to the punch, though without upsetting him or her too much. What matters at present is convincing yourself that you are as capable as you believe yourself to be when you are at your most confident.

12 SATURDAY   *Moon Age Day 1 Moon Sign Sagittarius*

You might be in the mood for Christmas shopping today, but save your money for another day to avoid making spur-of-the-moment purchases. Friends should be especially helpful and can offer you some timely advice. Make certain you listen carefully to what they are saying.

13 SUNDAY   *Moon Age Day 2 Moon Sign Capricorn*

You seem as though you are very duty-bound on this Sunday. It could be that family members are relying on you heavily and you won't want to let them down. Avoid rows by explaining yourself fully and allow younger family members to have more responsibility for their own lives.

14 MONDAY   *Moon Age Day 3 Moon Sign Capricorn*

Someone higher up the career ladder than you are can steer you in the right direction, if you are only willing to listen to what he or she says. Reliance on friends is strong and new pals could be formed around this period. At least part of your mind is now likely to be focused on Christmas.

15 TUESDAY
Moon Age Day 4 Moon Sign Aquarius

The 'lunar high' for December gives you everything you need to get ahead in a practical sense. The only slight problem could be getting others to maintain the pace you are setting. Active and enterprising, you give yourself fully to all new projects and show a positive response to work-related matters.

16 WEDNESDAY
Moon Age Day 5 Moon Sign Aquarius

It hasn't been like Aquarius to tempt fate recently, but that is exactly what you will be doing today. You are willing to take almost any sort of chance, because you know your own capabilities – and in any case, the excitement of the situation is what captures your imagination. Money matters should be easier to negotiate.

17 THURSDAY
Moon Age Day 6 Moon Sign Pisces

Emotional ties prove to be very powerful and this is a time when personal attachments mean the most. You are still active and enterprising, so will be looking for excitement. However, you are likely to be sharing adventures with your partner or family members you look upon with great affection.

18 FRIDAY
Moon Age Day 7 Moon Sign Pisces

You are in the mood for fun today, rather than being too tied down with the realities of work, and there should be many people around who are willing to join you. Stay away from negative people or individuals who are backbiting and cruel. The closer you are to the people you are dealing with personally, the better you will feel.

19 SATURDAY
Moon Age Day 8 Moon Sign Aries

Take some time out to think things through. Your mind is presently uncluttered with irrelevant details and you see clearly through to the heart of most situations. Reassure those with whom you live that you have been thinking about the festive season and that many of the necessary details are sorted.

20 SUNDAY
Moon Age Day 9 Moon Sign Aries

Some fairly interesting news is likely to come along and this allows you to address your own needs and wishes. Getting on with the task in hand is paramount, but there are so many distractions coming in from all quarters that this could be difficult. You definitely have one eye on the demands of Christmas.

21 MONDAY
Moon Age Day 10 Moon Sign Aries

Stronger than normal personal ego is likely under present trends. You might be taking on rather too much just now and a little fresh air would do you good. You need some space to think things through and to put the brakes on your present tendency to lord it slightly over others. This isn't usual for Aquarius.

22 TUESDAY
Moon Age Day 11 Moon Sign Taurus

Your powers of attraction are strong right now and that can prove to be very useful. The bearing you have on the thinking processes of those around you may be quite surprising and could lead you to taking the odd risk when dealing with your partner or sweetheart. You should throw caution to the wind in at least one matter.

23 WEDNESDAY
Moon Age Day 12 Moon Sign Taurus

This would be a good day for asking questions and for gathering new information about life and the part you play in it. Be careful with last-minute shopping. You could be fooled into thinking that you are getting a bargain, when you know in your heart that you are being conned.

24 THURSDAY
Moon Age Day 13 Moon Sign Gemini

Things ought to be working out reasonably well for you, particularly if you are working on Christmas Eve. Getting things to slot into place should be easy enough and you do show a great deal of respect for those with whom you work. Things at home are likely to be frenetic and none too comfortable on occasion.

25 FRIDAY
Moon Age Day 14 Moon Sign Gemini

You have a good knack for dealing with different sorts of people on this Christmas Day and show great adaptability. There is a slight restlessness around you and that means you will be happier to be on the move, rather than sitting in a chair and toasting your toes in front of the fire. Stay away from party games, because they will bore you now.

26 SATURDAY
Moon Age Day 15 Moon Sign Cancer

You need to tie up loose ends today and to get yourself ready for the end of the year bash. Resolutions are likely to come into your mind already, but you need to keep these as realistic as possible. Don't be too keen to alter anything today, but rather keep on your planning head.

27 SUNDAY
Moon Age Day 16 Moon Sign Cancer

You might receive a financial boost that could help you follow your own plans once the New Year gets underway. At the moment, this might represent little more than a promise, but it proves to be good news all the same. What it means beyond anything else is that those in positions of authority have confidence in you.

28 MONDAY
Moon Age Day 17 Moon Sign Leo

Energy levels are likely to be down today, thanks to the 'lunar low'. This really is the sort of day when you ought to be thinking about simple pleasures and good company. You are on the go for most of the time, so there is nothing wrong with taking a break.

29 TUESDAY
Moon Age Day 18 Moon Sign Leo

The Moon is still in Leo and that means the 'lunar low' continues to have a bearing on your attitudes and actions. As New Year approaches, you will be right back on form, but for the moment you are more likely to be watching and waiting. Anything with an artistic association is likely to please you today.

30 WEDNESDAY   *Moon Age Day 19 Moon Sign Virgo*

This is a day when you should be prepared to let everyone know exactly who you are. Once you have decided on a particular course of action, you are inclined to stick with it to the bitter end. New Year resolutions are still on your mind and you will be putting some of them into action early.

31 THURSDAY   *Moon Age Day 20 Moon Sign Virgo*

Things are speeding up. There are some great things happening on the social horizon and you ought to be in a good position to gain from them today. Any slight frustration that the holidays are preventing you from getting ahead in more practical ways will soon be forgotten once you are fully into the New Year celebrations.

AQUARIUS:
2016 DIARY PAGES

AQUARIUS:
YOUR YEAR IN BRIEF

As 2016 begins, January and February should be filled with opportunity and both months offer you the chance to get off to a really good start. At work and socially you should be on top form and you show the world what you are capable of doing, and just how unique you can be. You may also have a chance to get things done that have been waiting in the wings for ages.

It is highly likely that March and April will bring fresh opportunities, and these months should also be especially good when it comes to achieving your heart's desire in a romantic sense. Overtures you make to others at this time will not be misconstrued and you have the ability to break through difficulties and to get where you want to be. Take special care of friends at this time and also do whatever you can to support your partner in a new venture.

For Aquarius, May and June bring their own specific benefits, some of which are responsive to your quick wit and to a greater level of natural luck than you might have experienced before. The weather warms and so do personal relationships because by May you will be finding new love or consolidating present attachments. You may need or want to travel, and specific journeys should be rewarding.

Planetary trends look good for July and August. These are months of great movement and activity. Not only are you likely to be travelling more than has been the case earlier in the year, you are doing so to increase your enjoyment of life. New people come and go, but old friends will count the most. For some Aquarians a new love could be on the cards during August and you will make the most of this in a number of different ways.

You may need to be more careful during September and October. It isn't that you are doing anything wrong, simply that you don't have quite the accuracy of touch that you exhibited earlier in the year. As a result you may make a few unforced errors and require the help and resources of colleagues and friends. On a positive note, this is a great time for expressing your love and devotion and for planning ahead, specifically for the month of November.

For many Aquarians the final part of the year will be a mixed bag, although with the emphasis on continued success in personal and practical endeavours and an ability to get what you want from life. You need to be as flexible as you can and to give other people the benefit of the doubt. Christmas brings its own sort of benefits, many of which are family-related. You should commence the new year with a great sense of optimism and with some exciting plans in place.

January 2016

1 FRIDAY
Moon Age Day 21   Moon Sign Virgo

Be prepared to discuss things in order to enlist a little help. This will help you to get your plans off to an amazing start at a time when they stand a good chance of working out. Don't get caught up in red tape and, if possible, make sure that you can move in a certain direction before you put your skates on.

2 SATURDAY
Moon Age Day 22   Moon Sign Libra

A work situation could be enlightening and might lead to some unexpected advances. There are many surprises around at the moment which further bolster the self-confidence you have enjoyed since New Year. Your creative potential also looks especially good at this time.

3 SUNDAY
Moon Age Day 23   Moon Sign Libra

Travel ought to provide the real emotional highlights of the day and trends suggest that today will be a mix of business and pleasure. With everything to play for generally it looks as though you are being noticed by those who have it in their power to make your life easier and more comfortable.

4 MONDAY
Moon Age Day 24   Moon Sign Scorpio

At the moment, hearth and home offer you the best possibilities, and this trend will continue until later in the month. Although you are still doing what is necessary out there in the wider world, you feel most secure with what you know best. Be mindful of the opinions of your friends at this time.

5 TUESDAY · · · · · · *Moon Age Day 25 · Moon Sign Scorpio*

Friendship and teamwork matters are positively highlighted today and these are likely to play out in your social life. Make today your own as much as you can and allow the slightly competitive side of your nature to shine through, while remaining at all times one of the team.

6 WEDNESDAY · ☿ · *Moon Age Day 26 · Moon Sign Scorpio*

Your mental focus might not be everything you would wish today, meaning that this may not be the best time for major decision-making. Instead, allow others to make some of the running whilst you take a back seat. In many ways you are clearing the decks for the action you sense will be coming along soon.

7 THURSDAY · ☿ *Moon Age Day 27 · Moon Sign Sagittarius*

Today could bring high-spots where romance is concerned and you will want to make the very best of what the planets have to offer in this regard. Even if you are not involved in a romantic attachment at the moment it might be only a matter of time before something interesting comes your way.

8 FRIDAY · ☿ *Moon Age Day 28 · Moon Sign Sagittarius*

Keep your eyes and ears open to discover what is going on in your immediate vicinity. Even listening to gossip can be rewarding at the moment and might lead you towards actions that will see you better off in some way. New personalities could enter your life at this time and bring interesting interludes.

9 SATURDAY · ☿ *Moon Age Day 0 · Moon Sign Capricorn*

Heavy responsibilities may be the order of the day and you are likely to feel them keenly at some stage. Watch how you deal with loved ones at present and be willing to listen to another point of view. You can make gains but it will be hard to influence situations as much as you have recently.

10 SUNDAY ☿ *Moon Age Day 1   Moon Sign Capricorn*

In a contrast to yesterday, now you will probably feel at your most active and attractive. The slight hiccup that came along is well out of the way and you won't be stuck for an answer, no matter how much you are put on the spot. There are potential financial gains to be made owing to your present sensible thinking.

11 MONDAY ☿ *Moon Age Day 2   Moon Sign Aquarius*

The bigger you think, the better you will act today. This is the time of the 'lunar high', the two or three-day period each month during which the Moon occupies your own zodiac sign of Aquarius. You should be on the ball and can address almost any issue that comes into your mind. Be decisive whenever possible.

12 TUESDAY ☿ *Moon Age Day 3   Moon Sign Aquarius*

You may now find some good opportunities to build on past efforts and should have no difficulty raising your profile as far as others are concerned. It's obvious that things are changing because, in addition to the 'lunar high', other planetary trends are also beginning to offer you a new perspective on life.

13 WEDNESDAY ☿ *Moon Age Day 4   Moon Sign Pisces*

Fresh material plans can get underway today and if you have been thinking about making professional changes, this would be a good time to get on with them. You have a good ability to influence others without having to try too hard. Routines are dealt with in a flash, even if some of them annoy you.

14 THURSDAY ☿ *Moon Age Day 5   Moon Sign Pisces*

This is a favourable period for your love life and a day during which you want to stay warm and comfortable with your partner. The very best side of Aquarius is now on display and it looks as though you can call in a few favours from people who will be very willing to put themselves out on your behalf.

15 FRIDAY ☿ *Moon Age Day 6   Moon Sign Pisces*

There may be a personal triumph around now that leads to a great leap forward, at least in terms of your own ego. Even if you don't stand to make a lot of money or gain significant influence, what really matters is that you believe in yourself. The attitude of friends could be very surprising.

16 SATURDAY ☿ *Moon Age Day 7   Moon Sign Aries*

A loved one could prove rather difficult to deal with today and so, if possible, you should avoid getting involved in deep discussions. Your mind is now working on a fairly superficial level and you will enjoy the cut and thrust of social activities. Friends are less of a problem than relatives at the moment.

17 SUNDAY ☿ *Moon Age Day 8   Moon Sign Aries*

You will be able to get the best from social situations today and show the gregarious side of your Aquarian nature. Not everyone you meet will be equally helpful but you do have what it takes to talk awkward types round to your point of view. Your charming persona remains intact.

18 MONDAY ☿ *Moon Age Day 9   Moon Sign Taurus*

Don't be afraid to take the odd chance today, especially at work. You are capable, physically restless, and have great determination – all traits that others are almost certain to recognise. Action is the name of the game and you won't take no for an answer in situations you understand well.

19 TUESDAY ☿ *Moon Age Day 10   Moon Sign Taurus*

Trends suggest that this could be an inspirational sort of day and one during which you are able to achieve a lot, especially in relation to plans for others. Once again much relies on your ability to communicate and you have what it takes to turn heads when it really matters. Some small financial gains are also possible.

20 WEDNESDAY ☿ *Moon Age Day 11   Moon Sign Gemini*

Friendship issues and group encounters take up much of your time and you are likely to be quite gregarious in a social sense. This is a time during which you will be focusing on practical issues and the very best scenario would be to spend time away from home doing something exciting.

21 THURSDAY ☿ *Moon Age Day 12   Moon Sign Gemini*

It should not be difficult to get others to carry out your instructions, as long as you explain yourself carefully. The fact is that you would probably rather do things yourself, simply because it's quicker. However, there are times when you simply have to delegate and this could be one of those times.

22 FRIDAY ☿ *Moon Age Day 13   Moon Sign Cancer*

Although your confidence is likely to be high and you are still getting a great deal done, you might be fretting over money. Look at the situation carefully and you should discover that things are nowhere near as sticky as they might look. Get on-side with colleagues who you also count as good friends.

23 SATURDAY ☿ *Moon Age Day 14   Moon Sign Cancer*

There are likely to be some positive highlights related to family matters and you might be able to move mountains for others. This means there will probably be less time to address issues that are important to you personally but you are very practical and will be able to think up new schemes as you go along.

24 SUNDAY ☿ *Moon Age Day 15   Moon Sign Leo*

The 'lunar low' comes along, which is that part of each month when the Moon occupies your opposite zodiac sign. This can sap your self-belief somewhat and might make you prone to the odd mistake. Be bold and determined when you can, but also recognise the fact that there are limitations around just now.

25 MONDAY ☿ *Moon Age Day 16   Moon Sign Leo*

Temporary setbacks will arise at present but none of them have the power to hold you back for very long. By tomorrow you should be well on form again. Although you might have to tread somewhat carefully for today, you can still have fun when you mix with people you find stimulating and exciting.

26 TUESDAY ☿ *Moon Age Day 17   Moon Sign Leo*

Your ego is strong at the moment but that means it can also be easily dented. You would be well advised to avoid getting into any sort of row and need to be quite careful when involved in deep discussions. These could easily turn into pointless arguments – which will benefit nobody.

27 WEDNESDAY *Moon Age Day 18   Moon Sign Virgo*

Social and leisure pursuits probably demand more from you than you realise. This is especially true as far as your purse or wallet is concerned. If you use a little thought you can think up things to do that hardly cost you anything at all. What's more, these could turn out to be more enjoyable than any expensive adventure.

28 THURSDAY *Moon Age Day 19   Moon Sign Virgo*

Recent efforts begin to show fortunate results. Some of these may have been a little slow to come to the fore, but the pace of life is definitely increasing and you will need to keep your wits about you if you want to make the most of everything that is on offer. Don't forget about the needs of family members and your partner.

29 FRIDAY *Moon Age Day 20   Moon Sign Libra*

Others are inclined to listen to what you have to say so this is clearly a time to say what you think. Whether you will be quite as tactful as you might be remains to be seen but you should bear in mind the importance of diplomacy and keeping the feelings of others in mind. Attitude is also very important at work.

30 SATURDAY   *Moon Age Day 21   Moon Sign Libra*

Any headway you feel you have made so far this year may now seem less certain. This has more to do with your attitude than it does with reality so don't react too strongly. Rely on family members and friends to take some of the decisions at the start of this weekend, though by tomorrow you should be back on form.

31 SUNDAY   *Moon Age Day 22   Moon Sign Libra*

A confident gesture on your part makes others take more notice of you. This is no time to hide your light under a bushel and you really do need to shine when in any sort of company. You might be called upon to do something you haven't tried before, but nerves are hardly likely to get in the way.

February 2016

1 MONDAY
Moon Age Day 23   Moon Sign Scorpio

Events at work could turn out to be slightly more profitable than you might have expected. Apply yourself to whatever task seems to be most important but leave time later for having fun. The attitude of your partner could take some working out later in the day – so turn on your present Aquarian patience.

2 TUESDAY
Moon Age Day 24   Moon Sign Scorpio

Domestic matters are likely to keep you smiling and, with plenty to play for, the horizon looks pretty good. You should be chatty and approachable, as is usually the case with your zodiac sign, and you won't allow little problems to act as an irritant. This might be a good day for a short journey.

3 WEDNESDAY
Moon Age Day 25   Moon Sign Sagittarius

With your high spirits and a good deal of enthusiasm it looks as though you are ready for anything that life puts your way. Not everyone has your best interests at heart, especially in a professional sense, but you will know straight away if someone is trying to fool you in any way.

4 THURSDAY
Moon Age Day 26   Moon Sign Sagittarius

The focus right now is likely to be on romantic attachments, even though you are probably also very busy in a practical sense. You want to prove to the person you love the most just how important they are to your life and should have little or no difficulty in doing so at any time today.

5 FRIDAY   *Moon Age Day 27   Moon Sign Sagittarius*

There is much to aim for at work and ahead of the weekend you are probably also planning how you intend to enjoy yourself. Pace yourself as much as possible and don't take on too many jobs at the same time. Although little mistakes can be made today, none of them are of any real importance.

6 SATURDAY   *Moon Age Day 28   Moon Sign Capricorn*

An increase in your general level of luck can be expected around this time. This is likely to be especially true in financial matters, but this is not a good time for gambling or taking too many chances. You will instinctively know when you can chance your arm – it's all a matter of intuition.

7 SUNDAY   *Moon Age Day 29   Moon Sign Capricorn*

You are likely to find yourself busy and on the go and won't have a great deal of time to please yourself at the moment. Never mind, you are getting a great deal done and should be more than happy with your efforts before the end of the day. Friends should be very supportive now.

8 MONDAY   *Moon Age Day 0   Moon Sign Aquarius*

It now comes naturally to you to create bigger and better opportunities for yourself and there is nothing left of the shrinking violet you might have seemed to be a couple of days ago. Take all the power of the 'lunar high' and use it positively to make this an excellent period of advancement. The planet Mars is also especially helpful now.

9 TUESDAY   *Moon Age Day 1   Moon Sign Aquarius*

You could find yourself with more power at your fingertips and with plenty of people around who are willing to go along with your ideas and to lend a hand, progress is more or less inevitable. Your popularity is high and you may be a little surprised about how many people want to know you better.

10 WEDNESDAY
Moon Age Day 2   Moon Sign Pisces

Attracting the right sort of situations and people to your cause ought to be fairly easy at present and you have what it takes to win hearts and minds. You should also be very charity-minded at present and willing to do whatever it takes to make someone else's lot easier. Your popularity remains high.

11 THURSDAY
Moon Age Day 3   Moon Sign Pisces

You may need to compromise at work, especially as a lot of the ideas that are flying about at the moment are not at all to your liking. It's possible for you to disagree with others without being disagreeable and that's part of the hallmark of your present nature. Your best side is now clearly on display.

12 FRIDAY
Moon Age Day 4   Moon Sign Aries

When it comes to work and financial matters, present planetary trends suggest this will be a period of potential achievement and acquisition. If important decisions are required, slow down and take your time over them for the best result. Others may want to rush but that isn't your way now.

13 SATURDAY
Moon Age Day 5   Moon Sign Aries

Not only do you take pleasure from activities of all kinds at the start of this weekend but you are also likely to be surrounded by stimulating company when it seems to matter the most. You may feel contented, but you still need to apply some gentle pressure, especially regarding a family matter.

14 SUNDAY
Moon Age Day 6   Moon Sign Taurus

It is obvious that this is a period of fulfilment, especially through work. Of course if you don't work on a Sunday it could be difficult to make professional headway, but there ought to be time to plan your next move and to talk things through with interested parties. Don't get tied up with silly details today.

15 MONDAY   *Moon Age Day 7   Moon Sign Taurus*

If it seems as though certain strengths are lacking in you then the problem is likely to be that you are not looking deep enough inside yourself. Don't get too carried away with gossip or someone else's version of the truth. Remain dispassionate and make up your own mind. Your intuition is especially strong now.

16 TUESDAY   *Moon Age Day 8   Moon Sign Gemini*

Friends bring out the best in you and it looks as though you will freely become involved in co-operative ventures at this stage of the week. When it comes to taking decisions, slow and steady wins the race, even though a part of your mind urges you onward at a much faster rate.

17 WEDNESDAY   *Moon Age Day 9   Moon Sign Gemini*

Major initiatives and moneymaking schemes may be around but whether or not you decide to become involved in them today depends mainly on your overall attitude. The social trends are strong, so perhaps you should decide for yourself to dump some of the practical needs of the day in favour of having fun.

18 THURSDAY   *Moon Age Day 10   Moon Sign Cancer*

This is a time of strong intellectual insights and a period during which you are more likely to respond to gut-reactions rather than to simple common sense. When a little bell rings at the back of your mind it is time to pay attention. There could be some small financial gains for the taking, and today should be generally rewarding.

19 FRIDAY   *Moon Age Day 11   Moon Sign Cancer*

There is little that is beyond you now that your energies have reached something of a peak. Give yourself wholeheartedly to any project that captivates your imagination, whilst at the same time pushing for changes that you know are going to benefit you not only now but also in the medium and long-term.

20 SATURDAY $\qquad$ *Moon Age Day 12   Moon Sign Cancer*

The best thing you can do today is to get busy. Everything points to an active and enterprising time and you have what it takes to turn heads. Don't be in the least surprised today to discover that you have an admirer and don't even be astonished if you find out that there is more than one!

21 SUNDAY $\qquad$ *Moon Age Day 13   Moon Sign Leo*

The arrival of this Sunday isn't exactly breathtaking for you because the 'lunar low' is slowing life down somewhat. Take considered steps and, if possible, leave important decision-making until after tomorrow. It may seem that those around you don't have your best interests at heart just now, but it's also possible that you are being over-sensitive.

22 MONDAY $\qquad$ *Moon Age Day 14   Moon Sign Leo*

There could be an apparent decline in your fortunes but this really isn't anything to worry about. Difficult situations are temporary so you should not react to them more than is strictly necessary. Take on a job today that you might normally have left until tomorrow because by then you will be busy again.

23 TUESDAY $\qquad$ *Moon Age Day 15   Moon Sign Virgo*

Now you seem to have a good deal more confidence than might have been the case earlier in the month. Actually there is probably very little change – it's just a matter of your own attitude. One thing is certain: when you have to make decisions of any sort today you will not hang around jumping from foot to foot.

24 WEDNESDAY $\qquad$ *Moon Age Day 16   Moon Sign Virgo*

Don't take too much for granted today. You would be well advised to check and double-check all details and this is especially important when it comes to travel of any sort. You would enjoy getting away from things at this time and will be much inspired intellectually by almost any change of scene.

25 THURSDAY   *Moon Age Day 17   Moon Sign Libra*

You now have great power to change things, even if you do so in small increments. Although you are neither pushy nor argumentative, you can still get your own way most of the time. Beware of small mishaps later in the day because the Moon is not doing you any favours.

26 FRIDAY   *Moon Age Day 18   Moon Sign Libra*

Some quite interesting news is likely to come at the end of this working week and you could be whisked out of your usual routines by the invitations coming in from other people. Don't worry too much about domestic chores because you can catch up with them later. Stimulate your mind in some way.

27 SATURDAY   *Moon Age Day 19   Moon Sign Libra*

In terms of work you are in the middle of a rather busy phase and this tends to apply whether you work at the weekend or not. When you are not actually involved in your career you will probably be thinking about it, but you should also take some time to yourself and enjoy social possibilities with friends.

28 SUNDAY   *Moon Age Day 20   Moon Sign Scorpio*

Get some peace and quiet if you can for at least part of today. This may be a forlorn wish because it seems that the whole world has need of you at some stage. By the evening you might be happy to collapse in a heap – but even that desire is likely to be thwarted.

29 MONDAY   *Moon Age Day 21   Moon Sign Scorpio*

You can turn professional matters to your advantage at the moment and will be quite happy to look at new possibilities that could mean a change in responsibilities. Try to stay cool, calm and collected, even on those occasions when there is some provocation about. Routines are necessary, if somewhat tedious.

2016

1 TUESDAY
Moon Age Day 22   Moon Sign Sagittarius

There is little or nothing to stand in your way today and the amount of progress you make in life is at least partly down to your own attitude. Neither are you short of something to do, but this is a time during which you can easily tackle a number of jobs at the same time. Success is now much more likely.

2 WEDNESDAY
Moon Age Day 23   Moon Sign Sagittarius

Keep on the right side of those who are senior to you at work but do let them know that you are around. Your profile is high and the very likeable side of your nature is clearly on display. Don't get tied down with routines at the moment but stick to doing things you find interesting and stimulating.

3 THURSDAY
Moon Age Day 24   Moon Sign Sagittarius

Today should be favourable for adventure and travel – in fact there is an element of this cropping up all week. You won't find every job easy at the moment but when it matters the most you will be getting on quite well. Keep in touch with people who are at a distance and do your best to impress at work.

4 FRIDAY
Moon Age Day 25   Moon Sign Capricorn

There could be significant improvements where your professional goals are concerned and you should also find yourself in the right frame of mind to push ahead socially. There is plenty of energy around right now and you are determined to see things through. Social trends are good towards the end of the day.

5 SATURDAY

Moon Age Day 26   Moon Sign Capricorn

Your ego is strong and that means making an impression. Not everyone is going to understand the more forceful side of your personality because it is clear right now that you are not afraid to make decisions. Others are used to you hedging your bets, so a certain Aquarian is a little unusual.

6 SUNDAY

Moon Age Day 27   Moon Sign Aquarius

Examine your views regarding certain matters and ask yourself if you are being truly realistic. You are able to see through the haze that everyday life places over some issues and what you realise might surprise you. Enlist the support of relatives or friends if you find that you are out of your depth in any way.

7 MONDAY

Moon Age Day 28   Moon Sign Aquarius

Influences at work only highlight the need to think ahead and plan carefully. Routines can be something of a chore at the moment but in the main you are getting to your objectives in a fairly ordered way. If you have the confidence to speak out, you might make some advancement.

8 TUESDAY

Moon Age Day 0   Moon Sign Pisces

You can make great progress today, particularly at work. Although you might become distracted now and again you are still applying yourself very well in the main. Don't be in the least surprised if you discover that you have a secret admirer. This could be someone who finds it difficult to speak out.

9 WEDNESDAY

Moon Age Day 1   Moon Sign Pisces

Your mind is in overdrive and works much faster than would normally be the case. This might make it difficult for slower people to keep up with you, so you will have to be patient. You can't understand why colleagues or even friends are so slow in understanding things that are obvious to you.

10 THURSDAY
Moon Age Day 2   Moon Sign Aries

You can improve your general efficiency at this time and make material gains as a result. People you don't see very often are likely to be getting in touch with you around now and could easily have some interesting information to impart. Relatives are less easy to deal with at the moment than friends.

11 FRIDAY
Moon Age Day 3   Moon Sign Aries

You have the ability to delight just about anyone at the moment and since things are getting busy, you will be more content with your performance. Aquarius can charm the birds down from the trees at any time but right now you are even more approachable and friendly than usual.

12 SATURDAY
Moon Age Day 4   Moon Sign Taurus

You may feel it necessary to let others know the way you are feeling and that can mean speaking out when it might be slightly difficult to do so. The balance between diplomacy and honesty won't be easy for you to strike at the moment – but you will find it best in the end to stick with honesty.

13 SUNDAY
Moon Age Day 5   Moon Sign Taurus

Today your ego is in the ascendant and you need to be sure that you are making the right sort of impression on the world at large. In a professional sense this might be somewhat difficult on a Sunday but you won't have any problem at all getting onside with new friends or impressing the ones you already have.

14 MONDAY
Moon Age Day 6   Moon Sign Gemini

In terms of money you should now be entering a fairly stable period. There are gains possibly coming from directions you didn't expect and you should also discover that your general earning power is greater. There could be some special compliments coming your way this Monday.

15 TUESDAY   *Moon Age Day 7   Moon Sign Gemini*

You tend to be very forthcoming and comfortable in your relationships, both the general ones and romantic attachments. At work it is important that you make it plain you are capable of almost anything. On the way you could so easily surprise yourself with what you can do.

16 WEDNESDAY   *Moon Age Day 8   Moon Sign Gemini*

You will work very hard at present but not because other people expect you to do so. Aquarius is entering a very determined stage and you won't take kindly to anyone ordering you about. However, instead of reacting, which is simply a waste of time, simply carry on living your life the way that suits you.

17 THURSDAY   *Moon Age Day 9   Moon Sign Cancer*

You can expect a brisk general pace to life which is, after all, the way you like things to be. Less restrained by the actions or opinions of others, you push forward mainly under your own steam. There may be moments you need help but there is just a danger you will be too proud to ask for it.

18 FRIDAY   *Moon Age Day 10   Moon Sign Cancer*

When it comes to attracting money you are probably now in a better position than has been the case for a number of weeks. It isn't so much what you do right now that matters but rather the effort you have put in previously. Be careful, though, because cash can run through your hands like water at the moment.

19 SATURDAY   *Moon Age Day 11   Moon Sign Leo*

Slow down the tempo of events and be willing to accept second-best, but do realise that this interlude will only last a couple of days. You will automatically discover that you are in a more contemplative frame of mind so it's unlikely that you will feel particularly frustrated by present trends.

20 SUNDAY
Moon Age Day 12   Moon Sign Leo

You tend to enjoy the company of others at this time and will be doing all you can to socialise, even if the pace of life is slightly slower than you might have wished. There are many distractions around at this time and concentrating fully on the tasks that lie before you is going to be far from easy.

21 MONDAY
Moon Age Day 13   Moon Sign Virgo

This is a day during which you are able to call the shots and you won't ease up as far as the pressure is concerned until you go to bed again. It might seem as if this would be something of a trial but you clearly respond well to pressure and even soak it up like a sponge at the moment.

22 TUESDAY
Moon Age Day 14   Moon Sign Virgo

Now is a time to look forward to situations that make you look on the brighter side of life. For those of you who work, this is going to be a week that offers much of what you need in order to be content. Meanwhile, you find ways and means to keep family members happy and to sort out the mess some of them are getting into.

23 WEDNESDAY
Moon Age Day 15   Moon Sign Virgo

You are still spending a good deal of your time working hard but you also show a desire to change things to your advantage at home. It will have occurred to you that the year is growing older and the days getting longer. There could be significant incentives around to alter your home surroundings in some way as spring arrives.

24 THURSDAY
Moon Age Day 16   Moon Sign Libra

Family trends still look very good and there are small rewards coming in, probably of a financial nature and as a result of moves you made in the past. You could be just a little nostalgic on occasions and whilst there is no real harm in this you would do well to remind yourself that there is no future in the past.

25 FRIDAY *Moon Age Day 17   Moon Sign Libra*

Variety and warmth in equal quantities could make this day somewhat special. Don't get too involved with matters that have nothing to do with you and kerb that curiosity if you don't want to get bogged down in someone else's mire. There is enough to do today keeping yourself tuned in to what lies ahead.

26 SATURDAY *Moon Age Day 18   Moon Sign Scorpio*

Your thoughts are now set on widening your horizons as much as you can. Some of this has to do with work but there may also be a strong desire for travel. It might be difficult to go far for now, but you can plan ahead and for the moment even short excursions would do you a great deal of good.

27 SUNDAY *Moon Age Day 19   Moon Sign Scorpio*

Your mind is very sharp and ideas are flowing well for you at the moment. Active and enterprising, you also have what it takes to make money. At the same time you have to remember that this is a Sunday and that you owe some responsibility to the people you don't spend as much time with during the week as you might.

28 MONDAY *Moon Age Day 20   Moon Sign Scorpio*

Financial and practical matters receive a good boost from the planets, but you may not be in the right frame of mind to deal with them. Shelve things you don't want to sort out today and enjoy some time either alone or with one special person. Trying to bulldoze situations at the moment simply will not work.

29 TUESDAY *Moon Age Day 21   Moon Sign Sagittarius*

You will be very expressive and outgoing today. All traces of the hesitation and doubt that were evident yesterday have now disappeared and you know exactly how to get what you want in most situations. Aquarius is very attractive at the moment and that means you are in the limelight.

30 WEDNESDAY *Moon Age Day 22   Moon Sign Sagittarius*

You have a strong desire for personal freedom and can be quite fidgety if you don't get the chance to follow your heart today. Travel and cultural matters are of great significance right now and the strong intellectual qualities you possess make you shy away from anything that seems ignorant or lacking in finesse.

31 THURSDAY *Moon Age Day 23   Moon Sign Capricorn*

Current trends suggest that you can make the best of offers that come in from outside. These may have a bearing on your work and it is likely that you show yourself to be more than capable now – whatever you choose to take on. Romance is also on the cards for young or young-at-heart Aquarians.

2016

1 FRIDAY
Moon Age Day 24   Moon Sign Capricorn

This would be a very good time for important discussions and for making up your mind to get on with situations that have been waiting around for some time. You should discover that there is a great deal of help around when you need it the most and this may come from well-meaning friends.

2 SATURDAY
Moon Age Day 25   Moon Sign Capricorn

You should find ways to get ahead today, but now it tends to be in quite unusual ways. Give yourself chance to have a break as well because all work and no play can make an Aquarian a dull girl or boy. You shouldn't need to stand up for yourself much right now because others are doing it for you.

3 SUNDAY
Moon Age Day 26   Moon Sign Aquarius

You should find that Lady Luck is on your side at the moment. The 'lunar high' brings you new challenges but also supplies the wherewithal to deal with them. There are few mountains too high for Aquarius to contemplate at the moment and you have a great deal of determination to do what pleases you the most.

4 MONDAY
Moon Age Day 27   Moon Sign Aquarius

Now is the best time of the month for putting ideas into operation and for showing the world at large just how good you are at coming up trumps. Not only the 'lunar high' but a host of other planetary trends are working well for you. If ever there was a time for speaking your mind, this is surely it.

5 TUESDAY
Moon Age Day 28   Moon Sign Pisces

In a professional sense, things should now be going with a swing. If there isn't as much time to spend with your loved ones as you would wish, you can take heart because that situation is likely to be remedied later in the week. Someone who is above you in the pecking order could be especially useful today.

6 WEDNESDAY
Moon Age Day 29   Moon Sign Pisces

Various material objectives seem to have success written all over them at this time and you won't find it difficult to forge ahead, even breaking down a few barriers that might have seemed difficult to surmount previously. Give yourself a chance to shine socially by accepting what could be an interesting invitation.

7 THURSDAY
Moon Age Day 0   Moon Sign Aries

Your style of debate at the moment can be a little too sharp for others, which is why you ought to tone down your approach a little. Aquarius is usually one of the most diplomatic of all the zodiac signs, but that doesn't appear to be the case right now. Some patience may also be necessary when you are dealing with less than positive types.

8 FRIDAY
Moon Age Day 1   Moon Sign Aries

Someone in your daily life is likely to be influencing the way you are thinking at the end of this working week. Although you are still determined enough to make up your mind about most things, words of wisdom will stay in your mind and could lead you to modify a course of action that might be a little too radical.

9 SATURDAY
Moon Age Day 2   Moon Sign Taurus

You really will be in the mood to do your own thing today and won't take no for an answer once you have made up your mind about anything specific. If you sense that your ideas seem too outlandish for someone close to you, that fact could act as a red light. Maybe this will be no bad thing.

10 SUNDAY · *Moon Age Day 3 · Moon Sign Taurus*

The odd little personal problem might be on your mind and could possibly get in the way of smooth progress generally. You do need to focus at present and to have confidence in your belief that you are dealing with things as positively as you can. Make sure you finish one task before starting on another just at the moment.

11 MONDAY · *Moon Age Day 4 · Moon Sign Gemini*

This is likely to be an enjoyable day for you and it is possible to make the most of little opportunities that come your way. Generally speaking these will be more social than professional in nature. It is likely that people you see very rarely are either turning up now or at the very least getting in touch.

12 TUESDAY · *Moon Age Day 5 · Moon Sign Gemini*

This might be the best time of the month during which to reorganise your personal life in some way. Put your mind to work and take care of any details that you know need sorting out. Self-discipline ought to come easily whilst the Sun occupies its present position and you are certainly not afraid of change.

13 WEDNESDAY · *Moon Age Day 6 · Moon Sign Cancer*

On a mundane level this would be a good day to focus specifically on your work and on your longer-term future. Career issues may be the most important ones at present but they are not exclusive. Later in the day there should be plenty of time to think about having fun, which is also very important at the moment.

14 THURSDAY · *Moon Age Day 7 · Moon Sign Cancer*

This is a good time for building upon recent successes. You can consolidate your acquisitions and convince everyone that you know what you are talking about and can be trusted with greater responsibility. Your social life ought to be working out well, too, with a number of important invitations on the way.

15 FRIDAY   *Moon Age Day 8   Moon Sign Leo*

Significant news may fail to turn up during the first day of the 'lunar low' and you will probably be left to deal with situations instinctively. You will also have far less energy than was the case earlier this week, though what with one thing and another this might be an opportune time to take a break.

16 SATURDAY   *Moon Age Day 9   Moon Sign Leo*

Don't waste your time today on trivialities but rather make up your mind to deal with situations one at a time. Energy is still in short supply so it's very important that you pace yourself. By tomorrow the planetary picture will be looking much better again, but don't expect to move any mountains during this twenty-four hours.

17 SUNDAY   *Moon Age Day 10   Moon Sign Virgo*

This should be a most attractive time when it comes to friends and lovers. You are as charming as ever, anxious to please and filled with delight by the smallest things. Creature comforts will appeal and you have a strong desire to surround yourself with tasteful objects and people who stimulate your mind.

18 MONDAY   *Moon Age Day 11   Moon Sign Virgo*

In terms of your career you could be entering a week of fits and starts. If you really want to get on it will be important to deal with matters one at a time and to make sure each is sorted before you move on. Things are less problematical in personal attachments, which look entirely secure now.

19 TUESDAY   *Moon Age Day 12   Moon Sign Virgo*

Getting your own way with others ought to be fairly easy today, but you are also quite sensitive at the moment so you are unlikely to use those around you for your own ends. You can find ways and means to feather your own nest but will also be doing what you can to make the lives of others better, too.

20 WEDNESDAY   *Moon Age Day 13   Moon Sign Libra*

Your ability to communicate your true feelings to loved ones is very well-marked today. If you know very well that a heart-to-heart is long overdue, you could do worse than to instigate it sometime today. You have a light touch when dealing with subordinates or younger family members.

21 THURSDAY   *Moon Age Day 14   Moon Sign Libra*

You really do need to make room in your life for doing what you want, rather than what seems expedient. There are some interesting encounters on the way, some of which are likely to be totally unexpected. Don't be too quick to react to what sounds like an insult in case you have got the wrong end of the stick.

22 FRIDAY   *Moon Age Day 15   Moon Sign Libra*

Trends now move the positive focus on to your family life, and also bring you a real insight into the motivations of people in any situation. Your ability to predict how others will react may even make you appear to be a little psychic! This can be a very fortunate gift when it comes to business.

23 SATURDAY   ☿   *Moon Age Day 16   Moon Sign Scorpio*

Seek out pleasure and novelty wherever and whenever you can. You add to your stock of information now by being willing to ask the right questions and by focusing on matters that others find difficult to address. Any sort of puzzle or mystery is likely to captivate you both now and in the days ahead.

24 SUNDAY   ☿   *Moon Age Day 17   Moon Sign Scorpio*

It is likely that you will be in a dreamy and imaginative mood today and you may also be thinking about new ways in which to divert your mind. A restless steak is in evidence, though this can be dealt with by looking at matters that are new and interesting. What Aquarius seems to need most right now is travel.

25 MONDAY ☿ *Moon Age Day 18   Moon Sign Sagittarius*

Balancing your time commitments could prove to be rather difficult at the start of this working week. It will seem as though everyone is demanding your attention during every minute. This would be a problem to some zodiac signs but you have the mind of a juggler and can cope, even when the pressure is really on.

26 TUESDAY ☿ *Moon Age Day 19   Moon Sign Sagittarius*

This ought to be a fairly harmonious and happy sort of day, although you will continue to feel restless and have a strong need to ring the changes somehow. Rules and regulations might get on your nerves and you will be at your best when you are free to decide what you want to do moment-by-moment.

27 WEDNESDAY ☿ *Moon Age Day 20   Moon Sign Capricorn*

Today could be favourable for planning any kind of entertainment and also for getting out into the world beyond your door. Aquarians generally like the spring and a lot of fresh air is definitely good for you, so make the most of any good weather that is about. Even a short walk at lunchtime would be better than nothing.

28 THURSDAY ☿ *Moon Age Day 21   Moon Sign Capricorn*

You should not have to try too hard in order to bring others round to your particular point of view at present. With a generally charming attitude and a classless view of life, Aquarius is always at the forefront of activities and is usually very popular. Not everyone loves you today but try to ignore those who don't.

29 FRIDAY ☿ *Moon Age Day 22   Moon Sign Capricorn*

You could be of tremendous help to a friend or even a close relative today. There are strong aspects in your solar chart that emphasise your ability to both listen and to offer sound advice. Even if this means putting yourself out a great deal, you will help almost anyone who seems to be in a pickle.

30 SATURDAY   ☿ *Moon Age Day 23*   *Moon Sign Aquarius*

Your opinions count today – so much so that you may find yourself being consulted by almost everyone. You seek a place in the social limelight and will be surrounded by new possibilities in a professional sense. Beware of the danger of acting on impulse, even if this seems to be a way of life at the moment.

2016

1 SUNDAY ☿ *Moon Age Day 24 Moon Sign Aquarius*

You will enjoy being number one in a social sense and can use this Sunday to further your intentions at home and also with regard to romance. It seems as though everything you do is custom-made to get you noticed and you shine well in company. All of this should make you feel rather content.

2 MONDAY ☿ *Moon Age Day 25 Moon Sign Pisces*

Professional matters could prove to be a test of your patience, both today and tomorrow. Ring the changes when you can and avoid becoming too involved in situations you know cannot be easily resolved. You will be more temperamentally suited to dealing with these later in the week.

3 TUESDAY ☿ *Moon Age Day 26 Moon Sign Pisces*

You should find yourself in the middle of a very active period socially and there is plenty you can do to help yourself at this time. With lots of energy and a determination to see matters through to a satisfactory conclusion, you are able to address situations that looked quite daunting a few days ago.

4 WEDNESDAY ☿ *Moon Age Day 27 Moon Sign Aries*

Problems and obstacles can be quite easily overcome, with a combination of common sense and intuition. Working out the way others are likely to behave under any given circumstance should not be at all hard and you are able to contribute to the success presently being enjoyed by specific family members.

5 THURSDAY
☿ *Moon Age Day 28 Moon Sign Aries*

Someone may challenge you at work today, but you have a broad back at the moment and can deal with this sort of situation easily enough. Not everything goes your way right now but when it matters the most you have all the energy and determination required to get you to the winning post.

6 FRIDAY
☿ *Moon Age Day 0 Moon Sign Taurus*

This is one of the best days of the month for romance and you may now enjoy a special time with someone you love a great deal and easily find the right words to say to them. Beware of a slightly embarrassing situation if someone unexpected tells you how important you are to them.

7 SATURDAY
☿ *Moon Age Day 1 Moon Sign Taurus*

It is important to you to keep in touch with others today, and you might also find that the weekend brings introductions to new people. Educational matters should be going well, particularly for younger Aquarians, and there are likely to be romantic overtures of some sort, one or two of which could be especially surprising.

8 SUNDAY
☿ *Moon Age Day 2 Moon Sign Gemini*

Much of your energy now goes into fulfilling some of your ambitions, especially in a professional and practical sense. There should be time for simple enjoyment later in the day and it is important that you don't spend all day concentrating. Relaxation is vital by the time the evening comes along.

9 MONDAY
☿ *Moon Age Day 3 Moon Sign Gemini*

You tend to be more in touch with others now and can easily understand how their minds are working. This sort of deep intuition is typical of your zodiac sign, but this can also be somewhat uncomfortable on occasions because your empathy is so complete. Remember that you have your own life to live too.

10 TUESDAY ☿ *Moon Age Day 4 Moon Sign Cancer*

This is a wonderful time to be with others and to enjoy the positive trends that are presently surrounding you. You can be more or less certain to give a good impression and your popularity is likely to be high. If there is something you want but you have been afraid to ask for it, this would be the best time to have a go.

11 WEDNESDAY ☿ *Moon Age Day 5 Moon Sign Cancer*

You encounter the new and the unusual in almost anything you undertake at the moment and will be quite pleased to stretch the bounds of credibility on a number of different occasions. Don't held back by your perceived limitations but believe yourself to be capable of anything. You won't be, but it's a start.

12 THURSDAY ☿ *Moon Age Day 6 Moon Sign Leo*

Extra work seems to be the order of today but what is really happening is that the arrival of the 'lunar low' is making you look at things rather negatively. Allow others to take some of the strain and don't be too quick off the mark with new plans. It might be better to leave significant new actions until after tomorrow.

13 FRIDAY ☿ *Moon Age Day 7 Moon Sign Leo*

You could be rather suspicious of the motives of other people and that can make for a rather uncomfortable day in some respects. It would be best to give other people the benefit of the doubt, though without surrendering control altogether. Better astrological trends are on the way.

14 SATURDAY ☿ *Moon Age Day 8 Moon Sign Leo*

Current trends seem to be geared towards individual gain and although so far this won't have been the best month that you have ever known in a financial sense, things can improve a little now. Maybe you will discover that you are better off than you expected or it could be that some surprise gains are on the way.

15 SUNDAY ☿ *Moon Age Day 9 Moon Sign Virgo*

Your ability to communicate with others is stronger and so getting your message across is not at all difficult. Any form of travel would suit you fine right now and if you have decided to take an early holiday, then so much the better. Any journey, no matter how fleeting, works well for you now.

16 MONDAY ☿ *Moon Age Day 10 Moon Sign Virgo*

There are some interesting possibilities likely to come along early in the week but you may feel a little lethargic and not inclined to follow up on them. Take some time out to think things through and clear the decks for action from midweek onwards. Watch out for a particularly intriguing offer for travel later.

17 TUESDAY ☿ *Moon Age Day 11 Moon Sign Libra*

Beware of being too rash for your own good. The problem is that you are likely to speak out without thinking much in advance. This could land you in some hot water and you will need to react quickly in order to get out of trouble. Fortunately you are well equipped for thinking on your feet.

18 WEDNESDAY ☿ *Moon Age Day 12 Moon Sign Libra*

Much of May shows you to be less family-motivated than might sometimes be the case and you seem to be getting a great deal from friends, one or two of whom are making a return visit to your life. Many of the values you hold in common with others display themselves in quite a marked manner at present.

19 THURSDAY ☿ *Moon Age Day 13 Moon Sign Libra*

It looks as though you will have to deal with some restlessness that is rising within your nature at present. Staying put and concentrating on the same old things won't appeal to you at all. It could be the arrival of the early summer or simply a few significant planetary trends but whatever the cause, you need to move about.

20 FRIDAY ☿ *Moon Age Day 14   Moon Sign Scorpio*

A domestic relationship or some situation within your immediate vicinity is likely to become more of an issue today. You will require flexibility and understanding in order to deal well with others and need to exhibit more patience. Nagging doubts you feel today probably have no basis in fact.

21 SATURDAY ☿ *Moon Age Day 15   Moon Sign Scorpio*

When you are faced with something that genuinely interests you it should be easy to race for the finishing line but the same cannot be said of jobs that you see as boring or without purpose. Whenever you can, you are likely to leave such things to others but you need to be careful that you are not accused of laziness.

22 SUNDAY ☿ *Moon Age Day 16   Moon Sign Sagittarius*

Success comes quite easily to you today and you will be right on form, especially when in company. You relish the presence of interesting and informative people in your life and will be working hard to achieve specific objectives. Most important of all, you find it easy to concentrate now.

23 MONDAY *Moon Age Day 17   Moon Sign Sagittarius*

Work hard and decide in advance what your objectives for the day should be. Originality is the key to success and you are not short of that commodity. Personal relationships can prove to be very interesting at the moment and it looks as though you will discover an admirer you didn't know you had.

24 TUESDAY *Moon Age Day 18   Moon Sign Sagittarius*

Practical issues should be easy to deal with now and you show a great deal of tolerance when dealing with others. Colleagues are likely to be quite demanding but you appeal to their humanity and will be showing great sensitivity to the needs of others generally. Routines can be a drag but they may be necessary.

25 WEDNESDAY   *Moon Age Day 19   Moon Sign Capricorn*

New ideas and different perspectives are nothing new to the average Aquarian. Today you excel when it comes to looking at alternatives and you carry the opinions of others with you because of your powers of persuasion. Keep in touch with people who may be far away from you at present.

26 THURSDAY   *Moon Age Day 20   Moon Sign Capricorn*

Though optimism might seem to be in abundance, the fact is that you are somewhat hesitant right now. You will discover that you need constant reassurance from others and will be checking the attitude of family members and friends on a very regular basis. Get organised with family obligations.

27 FRIDAY   *Moon Age Day 21   Moon Sign Aquarius*

Your personal strengths put in a very definite appearance today and you should discover capabilities you didn't even know you had. Use the 'lunar high' to get ahead in any way you can but specifically concentrate on the possibility of advancement at work. By the evening you will simply want to have fun.

28 SATURDAY   *Moon Age Day 22   Moon Sign Aquarius*

This is the time of the month in which you focus on getting what you want from life. Your powers of persuasion are good and it should not be at all difficult to bring others round to your point of view. Although others in the family might be arguing, you play the honest broker and can do some important problem solving.

29 SUNDAY   *Moon Age Day 23   Moon Sign Pisces*

If there is something you want from a friend or a family member this may be the best day of the month to ask them. Not only do you have a good deal of cheek, you are also blessed with strong persuasive powers. Doing favours for others comes quite naturally and you will also be very tidy-minded at present.

30 MONDAY
Moon Age Day 24   Moon Sign Pisces

You are entering a week that has a great deal to offer socially and although you will be applying yourself very well at work, it is those hours you spend away from responsibility that are likely to be the most rewarding. Energy levels remain especially high and you should be quite sporting in your attitude.

31 TUESDAY
Moon Age Day 25   Moon Sign Pisces

Be bold, brave and determined when faced with some sort of challenge. This won't be difficult because you are clearly in the market for stretching yourself – though only when it suits your purposes to do so. You certainly will not take kindly to being told what to do by anyone today.

2016

1 WEDNESDAY
Moon Age Day 26   Moon Sign Aries

You are entering what is likely to be a reasonably good financial period, aided as you are by the present position of the planet Venus. Joint business matters are likely to go well and you will find it quite possible to come to mutual agreements with others. On a different note, you may have some slight problems with young family members.

2 THURSDAY
Moon Age Day 27   Moon Sign Aries

Today should put you in the picture regarding a specific objective and probably one that is of a personal nature. Your imagination might not be quite what you need it to be and as a result you will have some boring moments to get through. If time hangs heavy on your hands, seek out a friend in the evening.

3 FRIDAY
Moon Age Day 28   Moon Sign Taurus

You might be having difficulties with a friend or a social contact at the moment and if so you will be more inclined to turn inward towards your partner or family members. The attitude of colleagues needs some thinking about, but don't argue with them openly because that won't achieve anything.

4 SATURDAY
Moon Age Day 0   Moon Sign Taurus

There are social bonuses to be had at present. Others will discover just how charming you can be and the best qualities of Aquarius are now shining through. You are likely to be looking for entertainment and will gain as a result of your ability to lead the field when it comes to having a good time.

5 SUNDAY   *Moon Age Day 1   Moon Sign Gemini*

This can be a time of intuitive awareness and a period during which you can easily assess the way others are likely to be thinking and acting. Although there are some delays to be dealt with at the moment, when it comes to getting others to do your bidding you have rarely been more successful.

6 MONDAY   *Moon Age Day 2   Moon Sign Gemini*

Today is ideal for reaching out socially, probably in directions you hadn't really considered before. The attitude of some relatives could be rather puzzling and you will certainly have more success with friends than family members. Arrogant people may be especially irritating, so try to ignore them.

7 TUESDAY   *Moon Age Day 3   Moon Sign Cancer*

Career matters are on a roll at this stage of the working week and you can gain a great deal by simply being in the right place at the right time. In a professional sense you may be comparing notes with colleagues and will be in a good frame of mind to co-operate right across the board.

8 WEDNESDAY   *Moon Age Day 4   Moon Sign Cancer*

You could be somewhat too impulsive for your own good today and that means you must avoid taking decisions that will have a bearing on your life for weeks or months to come. Don't sign documents now unless you have no choice but if you must, make sure you read the small print as carefully as possible.

9 THURSDAY   *Moon Age Day 5   Moon Sign Leo*

You can feel a little low in yourself whilst the Moon is in your opposite zodiac sign and will have to work fairly hard to overcome the everyday obstacles that life places in your path. Don't overreact to situations you know in your heart are only temporary and plan ahead beyond the end of the week.

10 FRIDAY   *Moon Age Day 6   Moon Sign Leo*

You may feel lacking in energy again today and it will appear that everyone else is getting ahead much more progressively than you are. This is not really the case at all and is merely a matter of perspective. By tomorrow you are likely to be back on form so find ways to amuse yourself for the rest of the day.

11 SATURDAY   *Moon Age Day 7   Moon Sign Virgo*

This could well be a very good time to plan a day away, or even to take one at a moment's notice. You won't be happy to be kept in the same place all the time and can easily become bored with routines. There are potential gains to be made through casual contacts and unusual business deals.

12 SUNDAY   *Moon Age Day 8   Moon Sign Virgo*

Around now you could encounter some potential new friends and you should not turn down the chance to get together with like-minded people. The very gregarious side of your nature is clearly on display and you have what it takes to impress those who can do you some good in a financial sense.

13 MONDAY   *Moon Age Day 9   Moon Sign Virgo*

Try to seek out new social contacts at this time. This year is very important in terms of making new friends and you need to watch out in particular for people who are on the same intellectual wavelength as you are. There could be a stop–start feeling to today that can only be countered by applying yourself fully to the task at hand.

14 TUESDAY   *Moon Age Day 10   Moon Sign Libra*

You need to own up to your responsibility in a certain area of life, even though to do so might seem rather embarrassing. Getting your point of view across is not quite so easy now as it was a couple of days ago and it might seem that certain people are doing everything they can to get in your way.

15 WEDNESDAY *Moon Age Day 11   Moon Sign Libra*

Benefits are on offer today through relationships, and right now you should be feeling a safe and secure bond with loved ones. There will be time for romance in your life, even though you may feel that practical matters are not being attended to. Tomorrow is another day so for the moment simply enjoy being cosseted.

16 THURSDAY *Moon Age Day 12   Moon Sign Scorpio*

Instead of firing from the hip when it comes to discussions or even arguments, listen carefully to what others are saying. Compromise is possible and you will do yourself a favour if you accept this fact. Aquarius can be very awkward to deal with today but thankfully this is nothing but a short interlude.

17 FRIDAY *Moon Age Day 13   Moon Sign Scorpio*

You now tend to look towards those things that are both realistic and practical and in this way you make headway with your life generally. Aquarius is not always this sensible but it pays dividends when you are. Family members and friends alike should be clamouring for your attention at the moment.

18 SATURDAY *Moon Age Day 14   Moon Sign Scorpio*

Joint finances should be looking fairly good at the moment and your organisational abilities are also strong now. Life is likely to be fairly steady and your natural tendency to react positively to situations seems to be in place. Attitude is very important when dealing with professional matters.

19 SUNDAY *Moon Age Day 15   Moon Sign Sagittarius*

Though on a personal level you seem to be very boisterous, you also have it within you to be quiet and contemplative. This is a day that needs to be divided into compartments and a time when you can more easily come to terms with the attitudes and opinions of those with whom you live.

20 MONDAY *Moon Age Day 16   Moon Sign Sagittarius*

Today is good for communications and for getting to know people who might be of use to you a little further down the line. Be certain before you commit yourself to a major change and, in fact, it might be sensible to put such matters on hold for a day or two. Socially speaking you should be on top form.

21 TUESDAY *Moon Age Day 17   Moon Sign Capricorn*

Now you can expect favourable trends associated with travel of any sort and you should also be very sharp when in company. Your active mind goes this way and that and you respond very well to intellectual discussions and to anything associated with current affairs and your locality.

22 WEDNESDAY *Moon Age Day 18   Moon Sign Capricorn*

Taking actions without sufficient consideration will lead you to slight problems at the moment. You need to be very careful and to address new situations as cautiously as you can. The start of new projects will have to wait until you are sure that they are what you need in order to progress.

23 THURSDAY *Moon Age Day 19   Moon Sign Aquarius*

What could turn out to be the luckiest period of the month has arrived. The 'lunar high' offers you the chance to take a few chances and you should discover that your decisions tend to be quick and useful. Don't stick to routines at the moment but try to alter your schedules as much as possible.

24 FRIDAY *Moon Age Day 20   Moon Sign Aquarius*

You can have a tremendous influence over others at the moment and find it easy to bring them round to your point of view. It looks as though Lady Luck is on your side, which is why you are willing to take a few measured risks right now. Juggling work and pleasure ought not to be a problem today.

25 SATURDAY   *Moon Age Day 21   Moon Sign Aquarius*

Whatever you decide to turn your hand to is likely to be accomplished quickly and without any undue fuss. You will need to be on the ball when it comes to dealing with wayward family members later in the day but you also show significant patience now. What you really epitomise at the moment is effectiveness.

26 SUNDAY   *Moon Age Day 22   Moon Sign Pisces*

Optimism is now your middle name, even though the 'lunar high' is now finished. Steady and realistic but still able to move at least small mountains, the pace you are setting yourself is sensible and welcomed by others. Avoid getting bogged down with any sort of red tape.

27 MONDAY   *Moon Age Day 23   Moon Sign Pisces*

Certain information coming in from associates should prove to be very interesting today and you are likely to be up to speed in no time at all. Even the most casual remark can set you thinking and you seem to have what it takes to bring others round to your particular point of view without really trying.

28 TUESDAY   *Moon Age Day 24   Moon Sign Aries*

You will not be able to evade family responsibilities under present astrological trends and these are unlikely to weigh heavily on your mind. You take great delight in the successes that others are achieving and you will do all you can to support family members – especially younger people.

29 WEDNESDAY   *Moon Age Day 25   Moon Sign Aries*

It seems that you can get a great deal from a range of different people at present and you are unlikely to be looking at anything too deeply. The reason for this lies in the fact that there is so much around that takes your interest. You tend to be a 'grazer' at the moment, especially with new facts that surround your life.

30 THURSDAY   *Moon Age Day 26   Moon Sign Taurus*

Emotional attachments should now prove to be warmer and more secure than ever and you may not really want to move far from home today. Once you have made a move you will settle to whatever you have to do very well but will not show quite the flexibility of nature that often typifies Aquarius.

July

2016

1 FRIDAY
Moon Age Day 27   Moon Sign Taurus

There is more than one way to skin a cat and certainly so at the moment. You will need all your guile and cunning in order to get exactly what you want today, but there is help if you need it and plenty of people rooting for you. Make tonight special for your partner and be sure to pass on a few compliments.

2 SATURDAY
Moon Age Day 28   Moon Sign Gemini

Routines can be very displeasing this weekend so it would be great if you could simply do whatever takes your fancy at any particular point in time. Give yourself a pat on the back for a recent success but don't get blown away by it because there is some distance still to go. Consolidate your gains if at all possible.

3 SUNDAY
Moon Age Day 29   Moon Sign Gemini

You can now energetically get ahead with a particular plan of action and there won't be much to stand in your way. You should find most people quite helpful but there are likely to be one or two exceptions. People you care for a great deal are now in need of the special support you can offer.

4 MONDAY
Moon Age Day 0   Moon Sign Cancer

Creative activities are favoured at the moment and you will be in your element when you are actually making something. It could be that you are looking at the possibility of changes in and around your home and you certainly won't have to go very far away from your domain in order to find true happiness.

5 TUESDAY
Moon Age Day 1   Moon Sign Cancer

Present trends offer solutions to problems that have been a bind for some time. You show great clarity of thinking and have an ability to get to the heart of any matter almost instantly. Others will be envious of this talent but they won't be beyond picking your brains when it best suits their purposes.

6 WEDNESDAY
Moon Age Day 2   Moon Sign Leo

Progress is apt to be rather slow whilst the 'lunar low' is around, so much so that today and tomorrow mark a time during which you ought to be thinking rather than doing. Don't be too quick to take on anything new and you certainly should not be pushing the bounds of the possible until the end of the week.

7 THURSDAY
Moon Age Day 3   Moon Sign Leo

Keep to tried-and-tested methods of doing things because the new and radical is not the way forward at the moment. The greatest happiness today comes from being close to those you love, many of whom will be actively putting themselves out in order to make you happy. Routines might seem comfortable.

8 FRIDAY
Moon Age Day 4   Moon Sign Virgo

Those higher up the professional tree than you are might prove to be especially useful at the moment but only because of your own attitude, which is positive and helpful. Personalities are apt to enter your life around now and bring with them some interesting potential changes of direction for you.

9 SATURDAY
Moon Age Day 5   Moon Sign Virgo

Most friendship issues are positively highlighted and it ought to be a piece of cake to get others to do your bidding. Not that you are being selfish because most of your present intentions suit others as much as they do you. For most this will be a socially rewarding day, with plenty of romantic possibilities too.

10 SUNDAY   *Moon Age Day 6   Moon Sign Virgo*

There is the possibility of friendly get-togethers with others for many Aquarians as Sunday dawns. Stand by a decision you have made and don't be too quick to change direction just because a particular individual thinks you should do so. Don't get involved in family arguments at all.

11 MONDAY   *Moon Age Day 7   Moon Sign Libra*

Challenges and career moves are easy to deal with, and this is a time during which you don't mind at all taking on new responsibilities. You can be very impressive when in company so don't be surprised if others are paying you some significant compliments. Present trends are also good when it comes to love and romance.

12 TUESDAY   *Moon Age Day 8   Moon Sign Libra*

Good fortune seems to attend many of your efforts at the moment and you have what it takes to get ahead. Others are looking to you for support and inspiration and you are filled with energy that can be used in a number of different ways. New prospects are in store and you actively embrace them.

13 WEDNESDAY   *Moon Age Day 9   Moon Sign Scorpio*

It could prove profitable now to speak your mind. You will do so diplomatically and this means you are being listened to carefully, especially by superiors. Stand by a decision you have made even if this means working harder than usual but you also need to understand that flexibility can be a distinct boon.

14 THURSDAY   *Moon Age Day 10   Moon Sign Scorpio*

You will probably discover that you are the focus of positive attention from friends and new pals come along all the time. New interests will capture your imagination around now and there is no shortage of things to do. Your charm is in evidence and helps you to get what you most want.

15 FRIDAY
Moon Age Day 11   Moon Sign Scorpio

Sympathetic trends now surround family associations and you will actively want to spend time with your nearest and dearest. Today is excellent for entertaining at home and for making sure that friends are happy and content. Aquarius wants to be everywhere at the moment but works best from a sound domestic base.

16 SATURDAY
Moon Age Day 12   Moon Sign Sagittarius

It might seem in some ways that home is the best place to be for the first part of this weekend, though you won't take much persuading that this is not the case. If so you will be gadding about again and may take special pleasure from shopping or visiting a place of historic or scenic interest.

17 SUNDAY
Moon Age Day 13   Moon Sign Sagittarius

The emphasis at the moment seems to be on one-to-one relationships and you may be spending some time looking at how you can improve them. Family concerns are also likely to be uppermost in your mind and although you have what it takes to work hard, your mind may often be elsewhere.

18 MONDAY
Moon Age Day 14   Moon Sign Capricorn

Although most aspects of life should now seem fairly settled, your emotional responses might be somewhat odd. You don't get the messages from your partner that you might expect and could in any case be rather more sensitive than is good for you. Avoid taking things too seriously or too literally.

19 TUESDAY
Moon Age Day 15   Moon Sign Capricorn

Your general daily life might seem to take on a fairly routine quality and if you want any excitement you will probably have to arrange it for yourself. Do something different and unexpected, if only to keep others guessing for a while. The evening has good social potential but once again it's up to you.

20 WEDNESDAY   *Moon Age Day 16   Moon Sign Capricorn*

There seems to be a greater willingness to take the lead in romantic matters and although the middle of a working week might seem to be a fairly unlikely time to sweep someone off their feet, you do have that ability. You won't have much time for petty rules or officious people under present planetary trends.

21 THURSDAY   *Moon Age Day 17   Moon Sign Aquarius*

The 'lunar high' offers you the chance to get ahead of the pack and to make a good impression when it counts the most. However, you won't want to be spending all day doing practical things because there is fun to be had and you know just the right people to draw into your present schemes.

22 FRIDAY   *Moon Age Day 18   Moon Sign Aquarius*

Luck is on your side again and a few calculated gambles could probably turn out much better than you might have expected. A little cheek goes a long way and you have plenty at the moment. Your popularity is high and it won't be at all difficult to get what you want in almost any field of endeavour.

23 SATURDAY   *Moon Age Day 19   Moon Sign Pisces*

All varieties of partnership take on a new significance this weekend. These may be personal attachments, sporting associations or even business ties but whatever they are, the planets are shining for them. Getting along well with almost anyone is your forte and this fact certainly shows now.

24 SUNDAY   *Moon Age Day 20   Moon Sign Pisces*

In affairs of the heart, trends suggest you may now have periods of sudden magnetic attraction, which could turn out to be slightly embarrassing if you find yourself receiving an unexpected offer. Make your true feelings clear from the start in any contact with others or you may also inspire unnecessary jealousy.

25 MONDAY
Moon Age Day 21   Moon Sign Aries

Partnerships and affairs of the heart take priority now and this may also have a bearing on your working life. You will want to keep busy at the moment but might not have quite everything you need to take decisions you know to be of great importance. If in doubt, ask a colleague or a friend for help.

26 TUESDAY
Moon Age Day 22   Moon Sign Aries

Standard responses to others probably won't work today and you will have your work cut out wondering why relatives and friends are behaving so oddly. Perhaps you should ignore their behaviour and simply get on with your own life. Anything with a distinctly intellectual bent will attract you at the moment.

27 WEDNESDAY
Moon Age Day 23   Moon Sign Taurus

It looks as though you are now entering a much brisker period generally but with the Moon in its present position you will be quite committed to home and family too. The middle of this working week brings new incentives – though in reality some of them have been around a while and you simply did not notice them.

28 THURSDAY
Moon Age Day 24   Moon Sign Taurus

When it comes to social interaction of any sort, you are the undisputed master at the present time. Although there might be much to be done at work, it seems obvious that you would rather play. Seek out like-minded people for new projects and soak up the compliments that ought to be coming your way.

29 FRIDAY
Moon Age Day 25   Moon Sign Gemini

At this time, you should not be short of interesting company and the end of the working week for many of you brings with it some fascinating possibilities for later. Once work is out of the way set out to enjoy yourself. The evening can prove to be extremely entertaining, partly because you are at your amusing best.

30 SATURDAY   *Moon Age Day 26   Moon Sign Gemini*

Forces of change and transformation are at work in your life now. Since you are never afraid to commit yourself to the new and unfamiliar, this is unlikely to be a problem. Those with whom you live could have more difficulty with it, though, so try to smooth the path for them as much as proves to be possible.

31 SUNDAY   *Moon Age Day 27   Moon Sign Cancer*

Get an early start today with all-important projects and if you are away from work during the weekend, do what you can to put specific actions in place for next week. You won't be inclined to leave anything to chance, at home and at work, and this also includes important details relating to future travel.

August

2016

1 MONDAY
Moon Age Day 28   Moon Sign Cancer

Someone you meet today, probably in a professional capacity, can have a tremendous bearing on the way your mind is working. Today is not a time to stand on ceremony, but a period during which you have to tell the world at large the way you see things. You can be relied upon to use your present diplomacy all the same.

2 TUESDAY
Moon Age Day 0   Moon Sign Cancer

You may get the chance to enjoy a special time with a colleague today and have the ability to happily mix business with pleasure. Group situations work well in a professional and a social sense because all the sharing qualities of your Aquarian nature are now clearly demonstrating themselves.

3 WEDNESDAY
Moon Age Day 1   Moon Sign Leo

There could be a minor setback if you don't watch out today and as a result this is a time during which it would not be sensible to take too many chances with life. Listen to the advice of those you trust and settle for a low-key sort of day, though one that still offers a good deal of potential personal satisfaction.

4 THURSDAY
Moon Age Day 2   Moon Sign Leo

Your social life could be the place to look for successes today because you probably won't find them all that readily in a professional or practical sense. Friends should be warm and encouraging but there isn't really too much point in pushing yourself towards any chosen destination until tomorrow.

5 FRIDAY
Moon Age Day 3   Moon Sign Virgo

Your imagination might not be quite as well connected to reality today as is usually the case. If you are offered something that looks like a bargain that is too good to be true, turn all your analytical powers on the situation. You would be well advised to be as sceptical as possible around this time.

6 SATURDAY
Moon Age Day 4   Moon Sign Virgo

Certain tensions could arise at home, probably because of the way a loved one is behaving. Once you have offered your point of view there probably isn't much else to be done and you will just have to wait and see. Some of the best possible moments today come via friends rather than relatives.

7 SUNDAY
Moon Age Day 5   Moon Sign Libra

There may be times today when you can make a real difference to the way those around you are thinking, and this is particularly true with regard to work colleagues and past associates. Set out to have a good time. You might have been rather too serious for your own good of late and need to redress the balance.

8 MONDAY
Moon Age Day 6   Moon Sign Libra

Social matters should bring some promising new developments. You are friendly with just about everyone and more than willing to share what you have. Although there may be very slight hiccups in your romantic attachments, when it matters the most your partner or sweetheart is likely to come up trumps.

9 TUESDAY
Moon Age Day 7   Moon Sign Libra

Your imagination is easily stimulated around now and you won't have any difficulty at all following the possibilities that come about as a result of a daydream. When it comes to proving your case in an issue that has been on your mind for a while, what you need is evidence, and that might not be too available.

10 WEDNESDAY   *Moon Age Day 8   Moon Sign Scorpio*

Some objectives simply fail to materialise, which is why you need to keep your options well and truly open at this time. The attitude of friends or even relatives might be difficult to understand today and you will have to ask them to explain themselves if you are going to get on-side with them.

11 THURSDAY   *Moon Age Day 9   Moon Sign Scorpio*

The planetary focus at the moment seems to be quite definitely on the past and emotional influences are likely to crop up all the time. Anything that removes you from the limelight turns out to be a good thing because you are in a very contemplative frame of mind and, in the main, want to be left alone.

12 FRIDAY   *Moon Age Day 10   Moon Sign Sagittarius*

Try to avoid too much daydreaming at the moment because what you really need today is concrete action. A few rules might get on your nerves and you will be spending a great deal of time working out how to circumnavigate them altogether. Aquarius can be very mischievous at present.

13 SATURDAY   *Moon Age Day 11   Moon Sign Sagittarius*

With plenty to celebrate at home, you have what it takes to make this a really good day all round. Confidence isn't lacking when you need it the most and you are likely to be showing your friendliest face to the world at large. This is Aquarius at its best and it is something that others find distinctly captivating.

14 SUNDAY   *Moon Age Day 12   Moon Sign Sagittarius*

Exciting social plans should be on the agenda at this time and there isn't much doubt about your determination to have fun. Give yourself a pat on the back for a recent success but don't allow this to get in the way of your continued efforts to get ahead. Someone very special could be entering your life around now.

15 MONDAY   *Moon Age Day 13   Moon Sign Capricorn*

There might be some reorganising to do at the moment and if so you are just in the right frame of mind to take it on. The results ought to be more than worth the effort and you are steadily getting towards a new way of looking at old aspects of life. Allow a younger relative a little more leeway than you have been doing.

16 TUESDAY   *Moon Age Day 14   Moon Sign Capricorn*

All kinds of communications bring their own form of reward today. Be willing to talk to others and to make yourself available, even to those who have not always been particularly friendly in the past. Allow someone else to take on extra responsibility, particularly if it means a job won't get done otherwise.

17 WEDNESDAY   *Moon Age Day 15   Moon Sign Aquarius*

The 'lunar high' has a stronger part to play in your life today than was probably the case last month. Push ahead with your plans and use all the confidence that is presently running through you. People who come into your life around now could prove to be especially helpful in assisting you to get ahead.

18 THURSDAY   *Moon Age Day 16   Moon Sign Aquarius*

There are issues around now that should make your life a good deal easier in the future and what matters the most is that you recognise them. With a continuation of your renewed energy it won't be at all hard to take on many different jobs at the same time and to give yourself fully to all of them.

19 FRIDAY   *Moon Age Day 17   Moon Sign Pisces*

There is a good balance at the moment between the messages you are deliberately sending out, and the response you are getting in return. Not everyone is working on your behalf today but where it matters the most you can distinguish between the various motives in operation and react accordingly.

20 SATURDAY   *Moon Age Day 18   Moon Sign Pisces*

You will have your work cut out with minor duties and tasks today and so will not want to cloud your horizons by looking too far ahead. That's fine. You need to be sure that you have got all the details of life sorted and that you leave yourself with some time to think. This period has its advantages.

21 SUNDAY   *Moon Age Day 19   Moon Sign Aries*

It would be much better for all concerned if you let everyone know exactly how you feel today. Of course you will want to do so in a diplomatic manner, except in those cases when specific individuals really don't want to listen. With them you might have to be blunt and really speak your mind.

22 MONDAY   *Moon Age Day 20   Moon Sign Aries*

There are likely to be significant demands made on you professionally now. That could be one of the reasons why you choose to commit yourself mainly to family matters. Certain issues could look somewhat threatening and though you are not one to shy away from a challenge, accept that you can't be on top form all the time.

23 TUESDAY   *Moon Age Day 21   Moon Sign Taurus*

Communication with your partner or someone else with whom you have a particular affinity allows you to get to the heart of matters. In some ways this appears to make the present period a slightly more serious one. Nevertheless, there is plenty of time for flippancy and fun, even if you have to work harder than usual to smile.

24 WEDNESDAY   *Moon Age Day 22   Moon Sign Taurus*

It is towards personal concerns that your mind seems to turn now. Even though most aspects of your life should be running smoothly, you can find something to worry about if you try hard enough. If you are conscious that this is what you are doing, it would be best to find ways and means of diverting your mind.

25 THURSDAY   *Moon Age Day 23*   *Moon Sign Gemini*

Financial potential should be better than average today. If you keep your wits about you, you can certainly make the most of opportunities that come your way. Some advantage at work is also quite possible later in the day and by the evening your mind may be turning to more personal matters.

26 FRIDAY   *Moon Age Day 24*   *Moon Sign Gemini*

Personal relationships that have recently been in the doldrums need to be addressed more carefully now. Although you might still be finding it difficult to achieve the forward motion in your life that you would wish, there are definite signs that things are starting to go your way. Friends should be especially supportive.

27 SATURDAY   *Moon Age Day 25*   *Moon Sign Gemini*

Group related issues are now brought to the fore. These don't come hard to you with your easy-going Air-sign ways. Get any important work out of the way as early in the day as you can. Later on your mind is likely to turn in the direction of the weekend and all that you have planned socially.

28 SUNDAY   *Moon Age Day 26*   *Moon Sign Cancer*

Don't be surprised if you end up in the limelight today. Along comes a real boost to your spirits, even if you are mainly responsible for it yourself. Don't spend the day getting tied down with responsibilities that are not rightfully yours and put most of your effort into new starts and thrilling possibilities.

29 MONDAY   *Moon Age Day 27*   *Moon Sign Cancer*

It looks as though you will get on better today when you are mixing and mingling. If you are at work you will discover ways in which to combine business with pleasure but if the day is your own you will show yourself to be on top form socially. Find ways to prove what a truly romantic individual you are.

30 TUESDAY   *Moon Age Day 28   Moon Sign Leo*

You should now find that you are getting the most from romantic and leisure possibilities. More settled inside yourself than seems to have been the case for a few days, you are quite willing to watch others struggle, whilst you take a more contemplative and even matter-of-fact approach to life generally.

31 WEDNESDAY ☿   *Moon Age Day 29   Moon Sign Leo*

Practical matters could go somewhat off-course today but don't allow this to prevent you from pushing forward with determination. Many of your ideas will fall by the wayside but it's the remaining ones that matter. Move ahead one step at a time and when you know you have a winner, put in that extra effort.

September 2016

1 THURSDAY ☿ *Moon Age Day 0   Moon Sign Virgo*

Planetary trends show that social and co-operative ventures ought to be working out very well for you at the moment. Although there may be an issue to resolve early in the day it shouldn't be very long before you are working to the best of your ability and solving a few other problems on the way.

2 FRIDAY ☿ *Moon Age Day 1   Moon Sign Virgo*

A lift to your spirits comes along today and there should be some strong social highlights to be enjoyed. An arrangement that is likely to be made by friends might lead to some really interesting interludes, though it is possible that some of these won't actually arrive until later.

3 SATURDAY ☿ *Moon Age Day 2   Moon Sign Virgo*

Don't become overly idealistic about a romantic issue. It is possible that you are not seeing things quite as clearly now as would usually be the case and some impartial advice from a friend could be in order. Make sure your expectations of life are fairly realistic around this time.

4 SUNDAY ☿ *Moon Age Day 3   Moon Sign Libra*

Relationships could prove to be a little troublesome today. In your mind the fault is not yours but you are reasonable by nature and so will come to accept that it takes two to tango. Don't be too quick to make a judgement about a friend who is behaving rather strangely. You may not know all the circumstances.

5 MONDAY   ☿   *Moon Age Day 4   Moon Sign Libra*

A short phase of greater introspection and evaluation is now around and you will be quite happy to accept that you cannot always be noisy and active. You want to look at things closely and won't be so keen to push ahead with plans until you are certain in your own mind that they are going to work out well.

6 TUESDAY   ☿   *Moon Age Day 5   Moon Sign Scorpio*

Social matters tend to be helpfully highlighted and can lead you to a more progressive phase that is gradually likely to take over. There should be less internal confusion now and this diminishes even more over the next few days. Try to co-operate at work because to do so can be a definite boon.

7 WEDNESDAY   ☿   *Moon Age Day 6   Moon Sign Scorpio*

It looks as though you are going to be especially assertive and somewhat pushy today, a fact that could come as a surprise to your nearest and dearest. Aquarius is often as pleasant as the day is long, so on those rare occasions when you are pushy, those who know you best are naturally unsettled.

8 THURSDAY   ☿   *Moon Age Day 7   Moon Sign Scorpio*

Loved ones could prove rather difficult to understand today and a little extra effort on your part is clearly necessary. You might have to put the brake on some social activities for the moment or at least reorganise things in some way. At work you could make progress without even realising that you are doing so.

9 FRIDAY   ☿ *Moon Age Day 8   Moon Sign Sagittarius*

Someone may put the dampener on relationships for you, or at least they might try to. If you are aware of what is going on, you can also do something positive to prevent it. If matters appertaining to your love life are somehow up in the air, this would be a good time to sort them once and for all.

10 SATURDAY ☿ *Moon Age Day 9* *Moon Sign Sagittarius*

Your mind is sharp, making this an especially good day for study or detailed work of any sort. You will be able to come to terms with issues that confused you in the past and won't be at all lazy. Social trends continue to look good and some of the best possibilities come about as a result of a prospective journey.

11 SUNDAY ☿ *Moon Age Day 10* *Moon Sign Capricorn*

For most of today you will be feeling very positive about yourself and can make the best of impressions on the world at large. This is a Sunday during which you want to enjoy yourself and there won't be too much time for deep thinking. The future seems to be an unwritten book and for the moment you are happy to have it so.

12 MONDAY ☿ *Moon Age Day 11* *Moon Sign Capricorn*

You now have a great deal of energy available to put into whatever takes your fancy. Although there may not be anything particularly important happening at present, you are in a good position to enjoy yourself and also to bring a good deal of happiness into the lives of the people with whom you make contact.

13 TUESDAY ☿ *Moon Age Day 12* *Moon Sign Aquarius*

Now the brakes are really off. The Moon is in an excellent position to allow you to move forward with greater speed and determination than has been possible for quite some time. It looks as though Lady Luck is on your side and she could bring better financial prospects as well as new opportunities.

14 WEDNESDAY ☿ *Moon Age Day 13* *Moon Sign Aquarius*

Today is favourable for all sorts of new plans and for consolidating past gains in original ways. You are likely to be as sociable as ever and you show great flair when it comes to organising almost anything. Any negative traits of the last few days are nothing but a dull memory as you push forward on all fronts.

15 THURSDAY   ☿ *Moon Age Day 14   Moon Sign Aquarius*

You might be forced to fall back on your own resources a little today but that's no bad thing and you tend to cope with the situation very well indeed. You won't be too keen to listen to the advice of people you haven't exactly liked in the past but if what they are saying is the truth you would be mad not to at least take note.

16 FRIDAY   ☿   *Moon Age Day 15   Moon Sign Pisces*

You are likely to be getting the best from both career and personal matters now. Don't worry too much about details, most of which can be sorted out easily. If you feel tired later in the day, be prepared to take a rest and don't push yourself into situations that seem a terrible waste of time.

17 SATURDAY   ☿   *Moon Age Day 16   Moon Sign Pisces*

It looks as though you will be fully immersed in the social mainstream. You will be doing what you can to brighten the weekend, both for yourself and for the people you care about the most. You need to put in that extra little effort to get yourself ahead of the field, and could also be quite sporting at the moment.

18 SUNDAY   ☿   *Moon Age Day 17   Moon Sign Aries*

Where money is concerned, you could be heading for an extended period of increase. Although you might have to rein in your spending somewhat right now, this fact stands as evidence that you are looking at financial matters more closely. By next weekend you should find your position generally more secure.

19 MONDAY   ☿   *Moon Age Day 18   Moon Sign Aries*

It's time for some light relief, even though you may be almost entirely committed to your working life today. The practical joker within you is on display and most people will be happy to go along with your off-the-wall sense of humour. Aquarius is out for fun and this fact extends to your family life too.

20 TUESDAY ☿ *Moon Age Day 19   Moon Sign Taurus*

The emphasis today is on physical pleasures and a general upturn in attitude is quite noticeable now. With so many people gathering round to lend a helping hand you should not be surprised if many jobs get done in a fraction of their usual time. Plan now for an exciting period to come.

21 WEDNESDAY ☿ *Moon Age Day 20   Moon Sign Taurus*

You may not deal too well with criticism today and tend to be rather more sensitive than usual. This can be the case even if you are not being attacked at all, so before you fly off the handle you need to look at situations very carefully. Keep abreast of local affairs and get involved in community projects if you can.

22 THURSDAY *Moon Age Day 21   Moon Sign Gemini*

The focus for today is most likely to be on work and practical matters. You will be happy to talk to almost anyone and can be certain of eliciting the most positive of responses. Don't forget sporting activities and general ways of keeping physically fit. These are important factors under present planetary trends.

23 FRIDAY *Moon Age Day 22   Moon Sign Gemini*

Much of the fulfilment you experience today lies in private and domestic matters. It won't be possible for you to remove yourself from the real world altogether, but that is what you may feel like doing at times. This could be a response to the very active and even breakneck period you have experienced recently.

24 SATURDAY *Moon Age Day 23   Moon Sign Cancer*

It could appear that others are making too much of issues you don't consider to be important. Try to stretch your imagination and to see things from their point of view. Socially speaking you should keep life as simple as you can, and mix freely with just about anyone who comes along, chatting at every opportunity.

25 SUNDAY
Moon Age Day 24   Moon Sign Cancer

You may be entering a period of escapism. This isn't all that unusual for Aquarius but you need to be careful that you are not neglecting important jobs you have already started. All the same there is nothing wrong with being a dreamer now and again. You might even arrive at some significant conclusions.

26 MONDAY
Moon Age Day 25   Moon Sign Leo

With the 'lunar low' around today you could become somewhat disillusioned, though if you realise what is going on in an astrological sense you will also be quite aware that this is a very temporary matter. Stick to routines. These will suit you for the next couple of days and they offer a sense of security.

27 TUESDAY
Moon Age Day 26   Moon Sign Leo

Avoid making too many decisions again today and simply go with the flow. There are people around who can even make the period of the 'lunar low' a distinct joy but you have to give them the benefit of the doubt. Ask for something you want today because someone close to you is in a generous mood.

28 WEDNESDAY
Moon Age Day 27   Moon Sign Virgo

There are great opportunities around now for broadening your horizons in a general sense. Whether or not you choose to actually do anything specific today remains to be seen. Any opportunity to do something different is likely to be grabbed with both hands and you show a positive response to suggestions that friends are making.

29 THURSDAY
Moon Age Day 28   Moon Sign Virgo

The chances are that you will be ready to tackle any sensible sort of challenge today, so you should be in a position to know who is going to be on your team. The confidence to speak boldly in company certainly won't be lacking at this time and in many respects you are more dominant now than at any time over the last few weeks.

30 FRIDAY

Moon Age Day 0   Moon Sign Virgo

Professional developments may now be going just a little off-course, especially if you are over-committed in some way. Try to plan ahead, particularly if you are thinking of making any changes at home. A journey might suit you soon and if you haven't already arranged it, why not do so this evening?

October 2016

1 SATURDAY
Moon Age Day 1   Moon Sign Libra

Trends now place a major new focus on leisure and romantic matters. With everything working generally well you should be able to see quite easily how attractive you are to others. There are gains to be made at this time from simply being what you naturally are. Personalities abound, both at work and socially.

2 SUNDAY
Moon Age Day 2   Moon Sign Libra

Financial objectives can gain planetary assistance today so this would be a good time to look at money and to work out how best to plan for the future. At the same time there is a strong social quality to the day and you shouldn't have any trouble mixing business with pleasure.

3 MONDAY
Moon Age Day 3   Moon Sign Scorpio

A period of greater efficiency and higher energy is now on the way. With everything to play for, this ought to be a crackerjack of a week at work and you will be doing everything you can to make those around you as happy as you can. You realise instinctively at the moment that attitude is everything.

4 TUESDAY
Moon Age Day 4   Moon Sign Scorpio

There ought to be plenty of ways you can feed your ego at the moment. After all, it isn't a voracious monster as is the case with some zodiac signs. Nevertheless you need to be preened now and again and to know how important you are to those around you. Fishing for compliments might bring a bigger than expected catch today.

5 WEDNESDAY   *Moon Age Day 5   Moon Sign Scorpio*

If you have recently wished to make any sort of fresh starts, or improvements and changes to your home, this is probably the best time to get cracking. Enlist the support of family members and plan what you are going to do but, at the end of the day, it's really a case of taking the bull by the horns.

6 THURSDAY   *Moon Age Day 6   Moon Sign Sagittarius*

This is probably the best day of the month in which to express your love for someone very special indeed. Although you might be committed to work, you are also entering a period in which a sense of personal freedom is especially important. As a result you should try to arrange a break later in the day.

7 FRIDAY   *Moon Age Day 7   Moon Sign Sagittarius*

With your competitive streak now firmly on display you will want to push forward on all fronts. This might not be especially easy and you might need to use a little extra effort in order to get ahead of some of the small difficulties that surround you. Acting on impulse comes as second nature to you today.

8 SATURDAY   *Moon Age Day 8   Moon Sign Capricorn*

You are willing to work hard and to do whatever it takes to get to your chosen destination. Don't get bogged down with details today but stick to the main themes of life, because it's the big picture that counts. By the evening you will probably be quite happy to relax in the bosom of your family.

9 SUNDAY   *Moon Age Day 9   Moon Sign Capricorn*

Keep your eyes and ears open for useful input at the moment. There are arrangements to be made and some very good social trends on the way. For those Aquarians who have been looking for romance, this could turn out to be one of the high spots of the month, and you enjoy a new-found confidence.

10 MONDAY   *Moon Age Day 10   Moon Sign Capricorn*

This is a busy time, characterised by having lots to do, yet at the same time you probably don't feel very bright. The Moon is in your solar twelfth house, which more or less demands at least short periods of meditation and thought. Put a few routines on the back-burner and at least enjoy a relaxing sort of evening.

11 TUESDAY   *Moon Age Day 11   Moon Sign Aquarius*

Positive thinking really does pay off well today. The fact is that with the 'lunar high' bringing so much light and energy into your life, virtually nothing is beyond your capabilities. Something that has been at the back of your mind and which has been troubling you of late can now be addressed and settled.

12 WEDNESDAY   *Moon Age Day 12   Moon Sign Aquarius*

An element of serendipity shows itself in your life at the moment. Even without particularly trying very hard, you should discover gains coming along. The world is willing to help you towards your objectives and there is no doubt at all that a little cheek goes a very long way.

13 THURSDAY   *Moon Age Day 13   Moon Sign Pisces*

Focus your energies on constructing new securities, especially at home. Family members need your help and support so you should put aside at least part of today to show them the sort of consideration that is typical of your zodiac sign. Conforming to expectations outside of your home is less easy.

14 FRIDAY   *Moon Age Day 14   Moon Sign Pisces*

You may have to wise up on financial management today because it's clear that you haven't been taking as much notice of your bank account as you should have been. Don't worry, things are not likely to be as bad as you might first think and it would be fair to say that you are rather more pessimistic than usual.

15 SATURDAY   *Moon Age Day 15   Moon Sign Aries*

A period of significant progress comes along, particularly with regard to your personal plans. Specialist help is available when you need it the most and you shouldn't have to look far in order to discover your great potential. Popularity is also high, which is always an encouragement to you.

16 SUNDAY   *Moon Age Day 16   Moon Sign Aries*

New information is likely to put you fully in the picture and today allows you to make progress in many different areas of your life. However, much of what stands around you is only theoretical and much still depends on your own efforts. Fortunately, there are some very supportive planetary influences around during the coming week.

17 MONDAY   *Moon Age Day 17   Moon Sign Taurus*

Work and career issues tend to keep you on the go now, in fact you may find there is not enough time to do everything that you would wish. Keep an open mind when it comes to changes that are now on the cards and don't spend too much time worrying about what might happen. Most decisions will be yours to make.

18 TUESDAY   *Moon Age Day 18   Moon Sign Taurus*

There are some important things to do today but few of them will turn out to be quite as simple as you might wish. Still, it is possible to use a little concentration, just as long as you don't try to tackle too many tasks at the same time. A call you have been waiting for might come along later in the day.

19 WEDNESDAY   *Moon Age Day 19   Moon Sign Gemini*

Today marks a time when you will be busy enough but there ought to be moments for contemplation and for getting your head round problems that might have been with you for a while. Even casual conversations can offer significant clues as to your way forward in a practical sense and meanwhile you should find love to be inviting.

20 THURSDAY   *Moon Age Day 20   Moon Sign Gemini*

Along comes an influx of social invitations and some of these will detract from your ability to concentrate on strictly practical matters when they matter the most. Never mind, it's an interesting period all the same and being an Aquarian you need the stimulus that comes from interacting with others.

21 FRIDAY   *Moon Age Day 21   Moon Sign Cancer*

You may become more involved in domestic matters than has been possible for a few days. Your mind turns towards the needs that loved ones have of you and much of your spare time can be used to make others feel more secure. Leave a few moments just for yourself and take some time out to meditate.

22 SATURDAY   *Moon Age Day 22   Moon Sign Cancer*

In terms of money you should now be going through a fairly stable period and one that will allow you to deal with financial matters in a positive way. The real prospects for gain seem to be in the workplace and you have what it takes to make a good impression, with few limitations around to hold you back.

23 SUNDAY   *Moon Age Day 23   Moon Sign Leo*

Settling for second best is not usually your way but that seems to be the case at the moment. Routines can look quite attractive and you will plod along through the day in a reasonably happy frame of mind just as long as you don't push yourself too much. Try to maintain a good sense of humour.

24 MONDAY   *Moon Age Day 24   Moon Sign Leo*

Although part of you wants to push forward progressively, there are aspects of your mind that are restricted and far from forward-looking. Take on board the needs of those close to you and, if at all possible, enjoy a family day. Don't get involved in discussions that could so easily lead to arguments.

25 TUESDAY   *Moon Age Day 25   Moon Sign Leo*

You can be extremely persuasive under present planetary trends and should have very little difficulty persuading others to follow your lead. This can be especially useful at work, where advancement of some sort could be in the offing. The world tends to be the way you make it right now, so think big.

26 WEDNESDAY   *Moon Age Day 26   Moon Sign Virgo*

Things remain good for you in a social sense now and getting on with people who were difficult a few days ago should be quite easy. Routines could be tiresome, which is exactly why you tend to ignore them if you can. Artistically you are on top form and maybe this is a good time for planning changes at home.

27 THURSDAY   *Moon Age Day 27   Moon Sign Virgo*

There is one specific piece of advice that really matters today: get organised. You really do need to be on the ball and to prove to everyone around you that you know what you are doing and that you have a plan. Once people see that you are not simply bluffing your way through situations, co-operation is assured.

28 FRIDAY   *Moon Age Day 28   Moon Sign Libra*

Intimate relationships bring promising moments and should help the working week to end in a very favourable way. You have what it takes to win hearts and so if there is someone around you have been wishing to sweep off their feet it seems as though this would be the best time of all to give it a go.

29 SATURDAY   *Moon Age Day 29   Moon Sign Libra*

You need to keep things varied today. The more change and diversity you get into your life, the better you are going to enjoy what this Saturday has to offer. Leave all serious issues until another day and show how spontaneous you can be. You can also gain by simply being in the right place at the best time.

30 SUNDAY
Moon Age Day 0   Moon Sign Libra

It may not be easy today to see a point of view you basically don't understand, but it's only a matter of time before things are explained to you. It is probable that there are some events taking place right now to which you cannot be a party for the moment. Try to curb your natural curiosity a little.

31 MONDAY
Moon Age Day 1   Moon Sign Scorpio

Look out for new friendships on the horizon, a fact that may well please you at a time when present attachments might be in doubt. Don't be too worried if you can't get family members to follow your instructions today. Leave them to their own devices and get on with what is important to you, now that general trends are good.

November
2016

1 TUESDAY
Moon Age Day 2   Moon Sign Scorpio

Today's trends favour financial dealings of any sort, though you will need to keep your eyes open for people who are not quite what they might seem. If you have to sign any contract, be sure to read the small print carefully and be on your guard against any sort of fraudster.

2 WEDNESDAY
Moon Age Day 3   Moon Sign Sagittarius

There can be a great sense of both fulfilment and security around at the moment and you are likely to choose to stay close to home and family when you can. The attitudes of some of your colleagues might make work a less-than-wonderful experience but as always you tend to take matters in your stride.

3 THURSDAY
Moon Age Day 4   Moon Sign Sagittarius

A continuing trend that has a strong bearing on money matters might find you slightly better off than you might have expected. People are willing to put themselves out for you and will be giving you plenty of advice, even when you haven't asked for it. Be sure of yourself before you take any sort of risk.

4 FRIDAY
Moon Age Day 5   Moon Sign Sagittarius

It seems that you are now very concerned with making outright progress, especially at work. If you are between jobs at the moment this ought to be a good time to keep your eyes and ears open. People want to do you favours, though once again it's rather unlikely that all of them will be particularly welcome.

5 SATURDAY
Moon Age Day 6   Moon Sign Capricorn

Financial and business trends are going to be a slightly mixed bag. There is a strong tendency for things to seem unsettled and you may not feel totally comfortable in any specific way at the moment. Confidence grows with the day but you are not going to feel like trying to move any mountains right now.

6 SUNDAY
Moon Age Day 7   Moon Sign Capricorn

Current trends make it necessary to streamline your life in some way at the moment. Beware of spending more money than is necessary, especially on articles that you don't really want or need at all. When at home you feel settled and happy with family members, but strangers may present a slight problem.

7 MONDAY
Moon Age Day 8   Moon Sign Aquarius

Now a great deal has changed in the astrological picture of your life as the Moon races into your own zodiac sign. The hesitation is gone and you actively want to take chances. Your power to influence others is especially good and you know what you need to do to get ahead in almost any way.

8 TUESDAY
Moon Age Day 9   Moon Sign Aquarius

This would be an excellent period for telling someone how things really are. Although you might have been slightly shy of facing up to a specific individual, today is an exception. Stand up for what you believe to be true and you may be surprised at how willingly others defer to your opinion.

9 WEDNESDAY
Moon Age Day 10   Moon Sign Pisces

Put your mind to work and take care of any details that need to be sorted. The more you get done early in the day, the better are the prospects for social happiness later on. At work this would not be a good time to worry about your perceived limitations. Instead, hold to a belief that you can do almost anything.

10 THURSDAY · · · · · · *Moon Age Day 11 · · · Moon Sign Pisces*

Trends favour active communication today, so there is no point at all in sitting in a corner and waiting for life to come to you. Congratulations might be in order somewhere in the family and this would certainly be a good time to make a special fuss of a relative who has done well of late.

11 FRIDAY · · · · · · *Moon Age Day 12 · · · Moon Sign Pisces*

Your personality sparkles around now and there are lots of possibilities waiting in the wings. In some ways this is the best time of the month, because you have so much energy and a desire to please everyone. Don't worry if this doesn't work in at least one case because you are not a miracle-worker.

12 SATURDAY · · · · · · *Moon Age Day 13 · · · Moon Sign Aries*

Look out for very pleasurable social events around now, even though you are also likely to be quite busy if at work. There are gains to be made from simply watching and waiting, whilst at other times it is actions that count. Knowing the difference is really down to your very strong intuition.

13 SUNDAY · · · · · · *Moon Age Day 14 · · · Moon Sign Aries*

You may be able to take positive action to expand your financial horizons and trends suggest that you might gain as a result of someone else's mistake. Although you are looking closely at money, this isn't entirely the motivation of your life at the moment. Close personal ties are also on the agenda and you are doing what you can to strengthen them.

14 MONDAY · · · · · · *Moon Age Day 15 · · · Moon Sign Taurus*

If you branch out on your own you could make significant headway in some unexpected directions. There is much about today that feels original and you respond well to new offers that are coming your way. Avoid getting involved in discussions that lead nowhere.

15 TUESDAY *Moon Age Day 16   Moon Sign Taurus*

Your quick thinking could save the day now. There are gains to be made in a number of different areas of your life but romance is probably going to be the best of all. If your partner has confidence in you, then it seems almost anything is possible. Allow time today for having fun.

16 WEDNESDAY *Moon Age Day 17   Moon Sign Gemini*

There could be just a little luck in the financial sphere around this time and you need to be on the ball when it comes to any sort of deal that is in the offing. Look out for the odd practical mishap that is likely to be caused because you are a little clumsier than would usually be the case.

17 THURSDAY *Moon Age Day 18   Moon Sign Gemini*

Take a little trip if possible and make some changes to the routines of your life. It would be all too easy to become bored with things at the moment and in order to avoid this happening, you may have to put in a little extra effort. You presently show great consideration for family members.

18 FRIDAY *Moon Age Day 19   Moon Sign Cancer*

Communication with others is enlivening and even exciting at the end of this new working week. You tend to be acting on impulse for much of the time but this is so much a part of your basic nature that it isn't any sort of problem. Listen to the ideas of a colleague because they could suit you too.

19 SATURDAY *Moon Age Day 20   Moon Sign Cancer*

You are likely to be out and about more than ever today and the weekend offers much to those Aquarians who are genuinely willing to try hard. There isn't any use in waiting around for anyone else to make the arrangements, and although you will have to work hard to get others involved, the effort will be more than worthwhile.

20 SUNDAY   *Moon Age Day 21   Moon Sign Leo*

Today brings a lessening of your general spirits and vitality as the Moon enters your opposite zodiac sign. Keep your expectations reasonably low, even though in many respects you don't want to settle for second best. Attending to routine chores might seem to be the best way to spend parts of today.

21 MONDAY   *Moon Age Day 22   Moon Sign Leo*

Your capacity for getting ahead is still less than you would wish and a certain amount of frustration could be the result. Patience is called for, at a time when you don't seem to have much. Your creative powers are undiminished, however, and this would be an ideal time to do a little steady DIY.

22 TUESDAY   *Moon Age Day 23   Moon Sign Virgo*

You remain basically optimistic and committed to the future, though there could be the odd setback today and you will need to keep your wits about you if you don't want to end up restarting a project that is already underway. Try to settle for a fairly steady day, although that might be too much to expect.

23 WEDNESDAY   *Moon Age Day 24   Moon Sign Virgo*

Learning new things can be a great deal of fun at this time and you launch yourself into projects with a great deal of enthusiasm. Certain people could prove to be difficult and you will have to show great diplomacy if you are to avoid getting into some sort of disagreement or even a downright row.

24 THURSDAY   *Moon Age Day 25   Moon Sign Libra*

It is likely that you will be somewhat argumentative today and you need to curb this tendency if you want to avoid falling out with someone who is in a position to do you a great deal of good. Count to ten before you react and even when you are faced with people you see as being deliberately stupid you need to keep your cool.

25 FRIDAY
Moon Age Day 26   Moon Sign Libra

This should prove to be one of the better days of the month during which to enjoy friendship and the simple things of life. If you feel a bit lacking in sparkle all you probably need is a temporary change of scene. When a particular task gets boring or frustrating, put it aside for a while.

26 SATURDAY
Moon Age Day 27   Moon Sign Libra

Family and domestic situations are likely to prevail today. Get together with your loved ones and make some plans for the future. It is likely that one of your chief concerns will be Christmas, which is only a month away. When it comes to domestic chores, do your best to be inventive and to change the order in which you do things.

27 SUNDAY
Moon Age Day 28   Moon Sign Scorpio

Look towards a relaxing and interesting sort of day but also a time during which you will have to think deeply about an issue that has been on your mind for some time. Because you are quite laid back you can now deal with situations better and can find answers that have eluded you for a few weeks or even months.

28 MONDAY
Moon Age Day 29   Moon Sign Scorpio

Although those with whom you associate regularly think you are the bee's knees, this may not be universally the case. Don't be downhearted about this because you can't please everyone and you need to be the sort of person you really are. When it matters the most, people will come good for you.

29 TUESDAY
Moon Age Day 0   Moon Sign Sagittarius

This would be a very favourable time for all matters to do with holiday arrangements or even for planning a business trip of some sort. There is a degree of restlessness about you at this time and you need to bring some change into your life if you are not to end up feeling rather bored.

30 WEDNESDAY   *Moon Age Day 1   Moon Sign Sagittarius*

Take every possible opportunity to get away from the ordinary in life. Winter is here and things can start to look very grey and uninspiring unless you put in that extra bit of effort yourself. Aquarius has the power to lift its own spirits and those of everyone with whom it comes into contact.

December
2016

1 THURSDAY *Moon Age Day 2   Moon Sign Sagittarius*

The emphasis at the moment is on a broad-minded outlook, which is not at all unusual for your zodiac sign. Routines can be very useful but at the same time you are now looking well ahead and the prospect of what lies before you ought to be quite stimulating in more than one way.

2 FRIDAY *Moon Age Day 3   Moon Sign Capricorn*

Work issues should be going well at the moment, although you may have reservations and may not be quite as efficient in a general sense as would usually be the case. The realisation that Christmas is now only weeks away may not help because there is probably still a great deal to get done in an already busy time.

3 SATURDAY *Moon Age Day 4   Moon Sign Capricorn*

There are many priorities to be dealt with just now and once again you could discover that time is of the essence. Pass some of these tasks to other people. Friends in particular should be happy to lend a hand and want to do whatever they can to lessen your burden in life.

4 SUNDAY *Moon Age Day 5   Moon Sign Aquarius*

You may be able to successfully broaden your base of important social contacts now and these new people may play a big part in your future life. Doing half a dozen different things at the same time should come as second nature to you, and the planets also indicate that some small financial gains may arise from a little good luck.

5 MONDAY
Moon Age Day 6   Moon Sign Aquarius

Versatility seems to be the key to success around now and you won't have any trouble at all keeping up with the general flow of life. Although you might encounter one or two small stumbling blocks at work, in the main your progress is more than steady and at the same time social trends look good.

6 TUESDAY
Moon Age Day 7   Moon Sign Aquarius

Whilst you should find yourself pretty much on target with regard to your broad aims in life, there are possible little setbacks arising from the quiet streak within your nature. Maybe you don't have quite the level of confidence required to get things running your way practically or financially. The answer is easy – enlist some support.

7 WEDNESDAY
Moon Age Day 8   Moon Sign Pisces

Practical matters run smoothly and you should be contributing a very joyful attitude to whatever is going on around you at this time. Today would be favourable for organising and for getting an overview of where you are at the moment. There ought to be time for both extreme activity and relaxation.

8 THURSDAY
Moon Age Day 9   Moon Sign Pisces

Although personal relationships might be rather downbeat at present, you need to take your joys where you can find them. Today that means friendship and the support that particular individuals are offering. In a practical sense it would be best not to take anything for granted, especially at work.

9 FRIDAY
Moon Age Day 10   Moon Sign Aries

Friday should bring a period of swifter progress. If you put on a spurt you can steal a march on someone who has been beating you to the punch, though without upsetting them too much. What matters at present is convincing yourself that you are as capable as you believe yourself to be when you are at your most confident.

10 SATURDAY   *Moon Age Day 11   Moon Sign Aries*

You might be in the mood for some shopping today, but avoid making spur of the moment purchases and instead, save your money for another day. Friends should be especially helpful and can offer you some timely advice. Make certain you listen carefully to what they are saying.

11 SUNDAY   *Moon Age Day 12   Moon Sign Taurus*

Taking care of minor details will occupy some of your time today but you have a broader and more expansive interest in life too. This shows itself in a number of different ways, but as the day wears on you could notice that you are slightly quieter than has been the case for quite a few days.

12 MONDAY   *Moon Age Day 13   Moon Sign Taurus*

A person higher up the career ladder than you are can steer you in the right direction, if you are only willing to listen to what they say. Reliance on friends is stronger now and new pals could be formed around this period. At least part of your mind is now likely to be focused on the holidays to come.

13 TUESDAY   *Moon Age Day 14   Moon Sign Gemini*

Some fairly interesting news is likely to come along and this allows you to address your own needs and wishes. Getting on with the task in hand is paramount, but is occasionally difficult with so many distractions coming in from all quarters. You already have one eye on the needs of the season.

14 WEDNESDAY   *Moon Age Day 15   Moon Sign Gemini*

Although the sort of excitement you seem to be looking for at the moment could be absent, you can make it for yourself if you are willing to put in that extra bit of effort. Relatives and friends should be happy to join in and you can dream up some novel ways to entertain both them and yourself.

15 THURSDAY *Moon Age Day 16   Moon Sign Cancer*

Financially speaking, things now tend to look somewhat brighter. Of course any minor gains made at the moment are not likely to stay around all that long because the approach of Christmas is likely to see you spending fairly freely. Expect to wallow in life's little luxuries now if you get the chance.

16 FRIDAY *Moon Age Day 17   Moon Sign Cancer*

Daily life now has a brisk pace and although there are a couple of quieter days ahead, for the moment you need to apply yourself fully to whatever task you have at hand. Don't be too quick to judge a colleague or friend over an issue that probably looks a great deal worse than it actually is.

17 SATURDAY *Moon Age Day 18   Moon Sign Leo*

A little more thought needs to go into some of the decisions you are making at the moment. The fact is that the 'lunar low' might hold you back somewhat and as a result you seem to lack the sparkle that has been present for a number of days recently. Sit back and watch others have a good time if you don't feel like joining in.

18 SUNDAY *Moon Age Day 19   Moon Sign Leo*

You could do with keeping a fairly low profile today. This isn't because you are putting a dampener on things for others but merely because you are feeling a little below par. Routines probably work best and there is happiness to be found in your home environment. By the evening you should be on better form.

19 MONDAY *Moon Age Day 20   Moon Sign Virgo*

You are now very generous of spirit and far less timid than might have been the case for the last couple of days. Not only do you know very well what you want out of life, you also have a very good idea about the way you can get it. With everything to play for, you need to keep up with as many contacts as possible.

20 TUESDAY ☿ *Moon Age Day 21   Moon Sign Virgo*

Your best qualities now come to the fore and today ought to prove both rewarding and interesting. Risk-taking is on the agenda, even if these are fairly calculated risks. You have one eye on the Christmas period and in many respects this is the time when you really begin to get yourself into a festive mood.

21 WEDNESDAY ☿ *Moon Age Day 22   Moon Sign Virgo*

Your powers of attraction are strong right now and that can prove useful. The bearing you have on the thinking processes of those around you may be quite surprising and could lead you to taking the odd risk when dealing with your partner or sweetheart. In at least one matter you should throw caution to the wind.

22 THURSDAY ☿ *Moon Age Day 23   Moon Sign Libra*

This would be a good day for asking questions and for gathering new information about life and the part you play in it. Be careful with last minute shopping. You could be fooled into thinking that you are getting a bargain, when you know in your heart that you are being conned.

23 FRIDAY ☿ *Moon Age Day 24   Moon Sign Libra*

Take some time out to think things through. Your mind is presently uncluttered with details and you see clearly through to the heart of most situations. Reassure those with whom you live that you have been thinking about the festive season and that many of the necessary details are sorted.

24 SATURDAY ☿ *Moon Age Day 25   Moon Sign Scorpio*

Some of the pressures coming in from the outside world should lessen at this time and it is now possible to commit yourself almost fully to what lies ahead in terms of the celebrations. Aquarians generally love Christmas, even if a few of you try to pretend that this is not the case. Socialise whenever possible.

25 SUNDAY   ☿ *Moon Age Day 26   Moon Sign Scorpio*

Family relationships should be generally harmonious, one factor that allows you the chance to enjoy Christmas Day to the full. Join in all the party games and lead the celebrations whenever possible. One thing you might have to remember is to get enough physical exercise in amongst all the food.

26 MONDAY   ☿ *Moon Age Day 27   Moon Sign Scorpio*

Today could just bring a lessening of the amount of energy at your disposal. This really is the sort of day when you ought to be thinking about simple pleasures and good company. Being an Aquarian, you are on the go for most of the time so there is nothing wrong with taking a break.

27 TUESDAY   ☿ *Moon Age Day 28   Moon Sign Sagittarius*

Despite the holidays, this is a day when you should be prepared to let everyone know exactly who you are. Once you have decided on a particular course of action at present, you are inclined to stick with it to the bitter end. New Year resolutions are already on your mind and you will be putting some of them into action early.

28 WEDNESDAY ☿ *Moon Age Day 29   Moon Sign Sagittarius*

Domestic issues continue to be quite fulfilling and new social influences may help lighten the load if you feel that certain jobs are getting you down a little. With the New Year celebrations not far away it is just possible that you are tiring of having a good time. You do need to be quite organised at the moment.

29 THURSDAY   ☿ *Moon Age Day 0   Moon Sign Capricorn*

Present trends might incline you to become more egotistical than usual. You might also be taking on rather too much just now and a little fresh air would do you good. You need some space to think things through and to put the brakes on your present tendency to lord it slightly over others. This is not usual for Aquarius.

30 FRIDAY ☿ *Moon Age Day 1 Moon Sign Capricorn*

The more you put yourself about at the moment, the greater will be your sense of achievement. Although you might not be able to take the starring role in everything, you are unlikely to be moved too much by this fact. By the evening you should have your sights set on interesting social possibilities.

31 SATURDAY ☿ *Moon Age Day 2 Moon Sign Capricorn*

It looks as though matters connected with the past will receive beneficial highlights under present planetary trends. A chance to review some long-standing issues should not be missed, whilst at the same time you remain very committed to what lies ahead. New friendships could be formed in amongst the party atmosphere.

RISING SIGNS FOR AQUARIUS

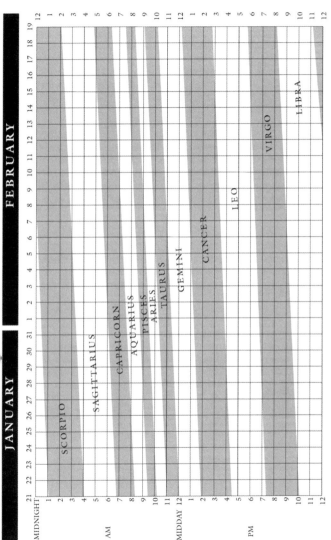

THE ZODIAC, PLANETS AND CORRESPONDENCES

The Earth revolves around the Sun once every calendar year, so when viewed from Earth the Sun appears in a different part of the sky as the year progresses. In astrology, these parts of the sky are divided into the signs of the zodiac and this means that the signs are organised in a circle. The circle begins with Aries and ends with Pisces.

Taking the zodiac sign as a starting point, astrologers then work with all the positions of planets, stars and many other factors to calculate horoscopes and birth charts and tell us what the stars have in store for us.

The table below shows the planets and Elements for each of the signs of the zodiac. Each sign belongs to one of the four Elements: Fire, Air, Earth or Water. Fire signs are creative and enthusiastic; Air signs are mentally active and thoughtful; Earth signs are constructive and practical; Water signs are emotional and have strong feelings.

It also shows the metals and gemstones associated with, or corresponding with, each sign. The correspondence is made when a metal or stone possesses properties that are held in common with a particular sign of the zodiac.

Finally, the table shows the opposite of each star sign – this is the opposite sign in the astrological circle.

Placed	Sign	Symbol	Element	Planet	Metal	Stone	Opposite
1	Aries	Ram	Fire	Mars	Iron	Bloodstone	Libra
2	Taurus	Bull	Earth	Venus	Copper	Sapphire	Scorpio
3	Gemini	Twins	Air	Mercury	Mercury	Tiger's Eye	Sagittarius
4	Cancer	Crab	Water	Moon	Silver	Pearl	Capricorn
5	Leo	Lion	Fire	Sun	Gold	Ruby	Aquarius
6	Virgo	Maiden	Earth	Mercury	Mercury	Sardonyx	Pisces
7	Libra	Scales	Air	Venus	Copper	Sapphire	Aries
8	Scorpio	Scorpion	Water	Pluto	Plutonium	Jasper	Taurus
9	Sagittarius	Archer	Fire	Jupiter	Tin	Topaz	Gemini
10	Capricorn	Goat	Earth	Saturn	Lead	Black Onyx	Cancer
11	Aquarius	Waterbearer	Air	Uranus	Uranium	Amethyst	Leo
12	Pisces	Fishes	Water	Neptune	Tin	Moonstone	Virgo